# Invisible Architecture

## The benefits of aligning people, processes and technology: case studies for system designers and managers

Jenny Ure and Gudrun Jaegersberg

**BCS**®

THE BRITISH COMPUTER SOCIETY

© 2005 The British Computer Society

The British Computer Society,
1 Sanford Street,
Swindon, Wiltshire SN1 1HJ,
UK
www.bcs.org

ISBN 1–902505–59–X

British Cataloguing in Publication Data.
A CIP catalogue record for this book is available at the British Library.

Disclaimer:
Although every care has been taken by the authors and The British Computer Society in the preparation of the publication, no warranty is given by the authors or The British Computer Society as Publisher as to the accuracy or completeness of the information contained within it and neither the authors nor The British Computer Society shall be responsible or liable for any loss or damage whatsoever arising by virtue of such information or any instructions or advice contained within this publication or by any of the aforementioned.

Typeset by Tradespools, Frome, Somerset.
Printed at Biddles Ltd, King's Lynn.

# Invisible Architecture

## The benefits of aligning people, processes and technology: case studies for system designers and managers

## The British Computer Society

The British Computer Society is the leading professional body for the IT industry. With members in over 100 countries, the BCS is the professional and learned Society in the field of computers and information systems.

The BCS is responsible for setting standards for the IT profession. It is also leading the change in public perception and appreciation of the economic and social importance of professionally managed IT projects and programmes. In this capacity, the Society advises, informs and persuades industry and government on successful IT implementation.

IT is affecting every part of our lives and that is why the BCS is determined to promote IT as *the* profession of the 21st century.

### Joining the BCS

BCS qualifications, products and services are designed with your career plans in mind. We not only provide essential recognition through professional qualifications but also offer many other useful benefits to our members at every level.

Membership of the BCS demonstrates your commitment to professional development. It helps to set you apart from other IT practitioners and provides industry recognition of your skills and experience. Employers and customers increasingly require proof of professional qualifications and competence. Professional membership confirms your competence and integrity and sets an independent standard that people can trust. www.bcs.org/membership

### Further Information

Further information about the British Computer Society can be obtained from:
The British Computer Society,
1 Sanford Street,
Swindon,
Wiltshire,
SN1 1HJ.
Telephone: +44 (0)1793 417 424
Email: bcs@hq.bcs.org.uk
Web: www.bcs.org

# Contents

List of figures and tables     vii

Authors     viii

Acknowledgements     ix

Abbreviations     x

Glossary     xi

Useful websites     xiii

Preface Jenny Ure and Gudrun Jaegersberg     xiv

Introduction     1

    Cutting risk and adding value in socio-technical systems     2
    What are socio-technical systems?     2

**1**   The problem with socio-technical systems     5

    A typical socio-technical problem scenario     5
    Implications for design and management     8
    Implications for design and management of socio-technical
    systems     10
    Further reading     11

**2**   Aligning social and technical systems to create value     13

    How can coupled systems create value?     14
    Digital repositories     14
    Strategies for aligning social and technical systems     15
    Strategies for sense-making and knowledge discovery     18
    Implications for design and management of socio-technical
    systems     19
    Further reading     20

**3**   Aligning knowledge and objectives in enterprise systems     21

    Portals: eBusiness     21

Implications for design and management of socio-technical
systems 28
The difficulty of aligning constructs and models 28
Implications for design and management of knowledge-based
systems 31
Further reading 32

**4** Cross-cultural architecture in the automotive supply chain 35

Aligning people, processes and technology in a modular
consortium 35
Aligning people, processes and technology in the supply chain 39
Cross-cultural potential for conflict: loyalty and impunity 43
Implications for alignment of people, processes and
technology in extended enterprise systems 45
Further reading 46

**5** Strategies for creating value in socio-technical systems 47

Using a common platform 47
Bridging the gap 48
Creating new linkages between technical and human networks 49
Aligning systems to create value 50
Further reading 51

**6** The architecture of human information processing systems 53

Information processing in natural systems 53
The Cognitive process 54
Implications for design and management of socio-technical
systems 59
Further reading 61

**7** Implications for designers and managers of socio-technical
systems 63

Seeing the invisible architecture 63
Implications for tools and training 64
Conclusion 66
Further reading 66

Appendix: Glossary of theoretical terms 67

Further reading 73

Index 81

# List of Figures and Tables

Fig. 0.1 Technical, social and organizational strands in the socio-technical whole

Fig. 1.1 Leveraging back- and front-end knowledge to create value for different users

Fig. 2.1 WebSOMs cluster information by a measure of semantic similarity

Fig. 2.2 Creating reusable, online resources

Fig. 3.1 Tensions in system design

Fig. 4.1 Diagram of an OEM's production line with integrated first-tier suppliers' production lines

Fig. 4.2 Incompatibility of different concepts of space and time

Fig. 4.3 German parent company: Coupled systems as shapers of organizational outcomes

Fig. 4.4 Invisible architecture: The cycle of behaviour-shaping in a Brazilian organization

Fig. 6.1 Knowledge as an adaptive interface between emerging information and action

Fig. 7.1 Typical supply chain improvement tools

Table 3.1 Aligning knowledge

Table 3.2 Aligning objectives

Table 3.3 Aligning expectations

Table 3.4 Situating recurring socio-technical problems within the context of the organization

Table 3.5 The conceptual relationship of various solutions to a core problem in systems design (over-capacity)

Table 4.1 Invisible architecture: The impact of cultural dynamics on standard business processes

# Authors

**Jenny Ure** has an MA (Hons) degree in psychology from Aberdeen, followed by postgraduate qualifications from Edinburgh University where she is now a Research Fellow. She has worked in a range of universities in the UK, Australia and Latin America researching, developing and evaluating collaborative, networked systems in education and business.

Her current research looks at knowledge management in the design and management of complex 'socio-technical' networks such as portals, intranets and supply chains in the financial services, software design, and the oil and gas sectors. She has a particular interest in strategies for the design and management of systems which align social, technical and organisational architectures to competitive advantage – 'building the technology around the social process'. She has published widely in this area.

**Professor Gudrun Jaegersberg** holds a chair in the Faculty of Economics at the University of Applied Sciences in Zwickau, and has worked in management education and industry in Germany, Italy and Brazil specializing in cross-cultural issues in globalization. She has been visiting professor to a range of universities in the UK, Finland, Italy and Brazil. She acquired her PhD in Humanities at Universidade de São Paulo, Brazil, and also has degrees from Westfaelische Universität Muenster, Germany and Bochum, Germany.

Her current projects focus on the area of knowledge management in the supply chain: she is currently managing a research project on the analysis of the soft processes increasingly seen as affecting the competitiveness of the automotive supply chain in Saxony, German and Paraná, Brazil. Prior projects focus on the development of new teaching methods using ICTs (distance learning) and Benchmarking in HEC.

# Acknowledgements

The authors are indebted to the many managers who have given their time, and for the support of funding agencies for some of these case studies. In particular we are grateful for the support of the UK ESRC, who funded the Socio-technical Patterns Project led by Prof. Ashley Lloyd at Edinburgh University and Prof. Rob Pooley and Dr Rick Dewar at Heriot Watt University. We are also grateful for the support afforded by a grant from the Deutscher Akademischer Austauschdienst (DAAD), and the Coordenação de Aperfeiçoamento de Pessoal de Nìvel Superior (CAPES) for the project on Knowledge Management in the German Brazilian Automotive Supply Chain. This was carried out in collaboration with Prof. Dr Hatakeyama (CEFET-PR/Curitiba, Brazil). We are also grateful for the many companies in Germany and Brazil who provided paid internships and technical and office support enabling 15 students to successfully complete a case study-based dissertation as part of their first degree. Case studies from Sandra Hoffmann and Gerd Schüler are drawn upon in Chapter 4. Thanks are also particularly due to Phil Murray of Petrotechnics Ltd (www.petrotechnics.com), who was extraordinarily generous with his time and his ideas, and to Matthew Flynn, Suzanna Marsh and Florence Leroy for great patience and generous support throughout.

# Abbreviations

ANT        Actor Network Theory
AST        Adaptive Structuration Theory
B2B        Business to Business
B2C        Business to Customer
CIE        Common Information Environment
CoP        Community of Practice
FIFO       First In First Out
HPC        High Performance Computing
ICT        Information and Communications Technology
JIS        Just In Sequence
JIT        Just In Time
OEM        Original Equipment Manufacturer
SSM        Soft Systems Methodology
STO        Socio-Technical Organization
UML        Unified Modeling Language
WebSOM     Web-based Self-Organizing Map

# Glossary

**Digital repository** An online library or archive of resources. These may be passive silos of collected information, or more adaptive systems which change in relation to input from users, as in the case of Amazon, for example, which draws on knowledge of the user community and the stored resources to recommend other titles.

**Extranet** Secure network used by companies to share business information and applications with third parties (other businesses, suppliers, partners, customers, intermediaries) securely across a public network such as the internet. Used as a secure private section of the internet.

**Global information system** A system of hardware, software and spatial data used for storage, retrieval, mapping and analysis of geographical data.

**Grid computing** A means of solving massive computational problems using large numbers of computers arranged as clusters embedded in a distributed communications infrastructure. Grid computing works flexibly across multi-user domains and involves sharing heterogeneous resources from different platforms and systems.

**Intranet** Internal network used by companies to share files, utilize websites and collaborate. This cannot usually be accessed via the internet.

**Middleware** Software that mediates between an application programme and a network. This facilitates interaction between disparate partners and applications.

**Portal** A site featuring commonly used sources as a starting point, or as a gateway to the web (web-portal). Typically these have search tools.

**Supply Chain** According to Christopher (1998), the supply chain is 'the network of organisations that are involved, through upstream and downstream linkages, in the different processes and activities that produce value in the form of products and services in the hands of the ultimate consumer'.

**VLE and MLE** The UK JISC (Joint Information Systems Committee) Steering Group points out that these concepts are still fluid, but refers to the components in which learners and tutors participate in online interactions of various kinds, including online learning.

They suggest that the related term Managed Learning Environment (MLE) be used to include the whole range of information systems and processes of the College (including its VLE if it has one) that contribute directly or indirectly to learning and learning management.

In effect, an MLE might consist of a whole range of different software and systems that interrelate, share data and contribute to learning management. A VLE refers to a specific piece of software that enables learners and staff to interact, and includes content delivery and tracking.

Diagrammatic explanation and further details are available on ferl.becta.org.uk/display.cfm?page=248

# Useful Websites

**Decision support software** based on construct theory. Used to support the management of soft issues by creating shared representations of ideas that can then be explored by the decision-making group.
www.banxia.com

**Knowledge management company** servicing oil and gas majors. Petro-technics is a global leader in the development and operation of safe systems at work.
www.petrotechnics.com

**Large digital image archive** providing web-based tools and services for users to customize the system and the resources around individual or organizational requirements.
www.scran.ac.uk

**Self-organizing maps** used to map information in cognitively intuitive ways.
websom.hut.fi/websom/

**The British Computer Society Sociotechnical Group** supports a pro-gramme of socio-technically based research, analysis, and education and lectures. The site includes both upcoming events and the text of past lectures.
www.sociotechnical.org

**Socio-technical patterns in organisations.**
www.bell-labs.com/cgi-user/OrgPatterns/OrgPatterns

# Preface

When the same technology produces different results across operating sites, you know there is another dynamic in operation. This book describes the invisible architecture of those dynamics in some of their most familiar and recurrent forms.

The scenarios are real ones, from contexts as diverse as defence, manufacturing, engineering, ebusiness and virtual learning environments, and highlight the problems that most typically impacted on cost, quality and performance in extended enterprise systems.

The intention is to generate an awareness of the invisible structures and forces in human information systems, and the extent to which this offers both an opportunity and a challenge for system designers and managers.

The book highlights the extent to which these less tangible forces can be harnessed to advantage through design that builds on this invisible architecture. It also flags the potential for cost and risk where technical and human information systems work in opposition to each other.

Case studies are used, rather than theory, to highlight strategies that have practical applications for system designers and system managers facing the growing raft of socio-technical problems that are a feature of today's extended enterprises.

Jenny Ure and Gudrun Jaegersberg

# Introduction

*We know how to deal with the technology. It's the people that are the problem.*

*CEO, oil and gas supply chain consultancy*

Everyone has had the experience of starting a new job and thinking they understand the way it works from the initial job specification, only to find that very different structures and dynamics are also in operation, and that this presents hidden (but very real) dangers for the uninitiated. A tacit knowledge of the invisible barriers and conduits allows those in the know to manage outcomes effectively. Such processes shape the performance of social and socio-technical systems in ways that require consideration by designers and managers mindful of the need to minimize potential cost and risk, and the need to optimize performance across sites.

A concern with people issues, expressed clearly in many organizations, underlines a growing need for senior technical managers to have well-developed strategies for non-technical issues, as the focus of much information and communications technology (ICT) design relates to the migration of organizational processes onto web-based systems designed to extend the range of business to business (B2B) and business to customer (B2C) transactions across an increasing number of networked communities. Both designers and managers have a part to play in creating the processes and the systems that are the vehicles for creating socio-technical synergy.

Designers and managers of portals, extranets and supply chains increasingly express concerns about the impact of these intangible socio-technical problems on performance. In interviews, we were struck by the consistency with which technical managers raised the same concerns, across different industry sectors and different types networks:

- unpredicted costs and risks where apparently standard technical and business systems are not compatible with local ones;

- lack of training in handling the soft processes that impact on the competitiveness of extended enterprise systems;

- lack of management tools for mapping and managing these non-technical problems.

## CUTTING RISK AND ADDING VALUE IN SOCIO-TECHNICAL SYSTEMS

The cases here highlight recurring problems identified in interviews with managers across a broad spectrum of industries, focusing particularly on the need to align people, processes and technologies to greater advantage.

We use the term socio-technical for the sake of simplicity, but refer here to the interfaces between technical systems and the many layers of human architectures – from cognitive systems underpinning perception and understanding, to the socio-cultural systems of local communities, to the wider architecture of the socio-political, socio-economic and socio-cultural systems in which they operate.

The first example in Chapter 1 describes a generic socio-technical problem, to give the reader a sense of the socio-technical issues in context. It is followed by examples of recurrent problems and strategic principles drawn from different industry sectors. Finally all the scenarios are drawn together in a summary of strategies for aligning technical and human systems, including a short overview of how human systems process information and manage knowledge

## WHAT ARE SOCIO-TECHNICAL SYSTEMS?

Cliff Joslyn and Luis Rocha at Los Alamos National Labs describe socio-technical organizations (STOs) as organizations that 'involve the interaction of physical systems that are "deterministic" with human systems (cognitive, social, organizational, cultural, economic or political, for example) which are less so'. This definition highlights a defining problem – the fact that the architecture of human information systems is variable and constantly adapted to the local environment, while the architecture of technical information systems is standardized and less adaptive.

These go from cognitive networks, up to the social/cultural/organizational networks that structure society and shape outcomes. Networked business systems have both a technical and a human component, in which dynamic forces may be at odds, or in synchrony. In such systems, the different strands can be differently constructed or aligned, resulting in performance differences even where the same technology is being used.

Technology increasingly supports working relationships with external groups whose cooperation is central to competitiveness, such as first-, second- and third-tier suppliers, companies to whom aspects of a business have been outsourced, and staff in partner organizations. As technology extends the potential for collaborative partnerships, it extends the need for understanding how these interrelated social, organizational and culturally defined processes can be mapped and managed.

FIGURE **0.1** *Technical, social and organizational strands in the socio-technical whole*

Many authors have contributed to the development of the concept of socio-technical systems, from the early work of Mumford, Pasmore and Trist to more recent authors such as Wanda Orlikowski who emphasized the interaction of technical and human processes in the design and management of extended enterprise systems. While discussion is limited to the cases described here, we have highlighted relevant authors in the sections for further reading for those who wish to follow up the associated theoretical positions in more detail.

# 1 The Problem with Socio-technical Systems

*Software designed to standardise safety compliance procedures globally, was actually increasing risk in some local operating sites.*

*CEO, safety compliance software company*

How can different systems work together to create value rather than chaos? The technical architecture of business systems may be standardized across a distributed network, the associated human architecture of users and operators is not. In many networked systems (e.g. intranet, portal, supply chain) staff are used to solving technology-related problems, but when people issues arise, individuals in the company feel less well equipped, and knowledge of how they manage these dynamics is less accessible. These problems were repeated to us by CEOs and senior managers in different industry sectors in extended enterprises operating over multiple sectors. They indicated concerns that success in the design and management of complex B2B and B2C transactions was more than a technical issue and posed challenges to performance levels and competitiveness that they needed to address more effectively.

The examples we give in the book highlight the extent to which technical and social systems are inextricably coupled in extended enterprise systems, and suggest strategies used to align these to mutual advantage. In providing them we hope it is apparent that there are a core of generic scenarios common to system design anywhere, and some recurring strategies for aligning the technical and the human resource to advantage. The case that follows is intended to give an introduction to what we mean by the term socio-technical in practical terms. It is also one of the most recurrent scenarios, having been identified across multiple sectors in different guises.

## A TYPICAL SOCIO-TECHNICAL PROBLEM SCENARIO

Among the many managers interviewed, we encountered an astonishing uniformity of concerns around very recognizable, and apparently generic, problems. One of the most fundamental problems, occurring in varying guises, is what we have termed the 'local: global' problem. This example of knowledge management software from the oil and gas industry highlights the problem in context and one strategic approach to resolving it. In doing so it illustrates some of the socio-technical issues associated with designing or managing systems that must leverage diverse, distributed human resources to cut cost/risk and add value in volatile, competitive markets. It also shows the importance of understanding interrelated or coupled processes, and developing strategies for harnessing them to advantage – knowing that those same forces can also be destructive if ignored.

## CASE 1: ALIGNING LOCAL AND GLOBAL REQUIREMENTS

### STANDARDIZING SYSTEMS IN THE SUPPLY CHAIN

#### Context

This case comes from an award-winning knowledge management company (Petrotechnics, www.petrotechnics.com) providing safety compliance software systems to a number of companies in the oil and gas industry. It deals with the difficulty of both designing and subsequently managing the implementation of safety compliance software and standardized procedures across a very widely distributed and heterogeneous set of collaborating operators in the supply chain.

The *intention* was to meet standard specifications for services and procedures across operations in several countries.

The *assumption*, albeit tacit, was that standardizing safety compliance procedures would improve safety and cut risk.

#### Problem of Alignment

The problem arose when it became apparent that the standard procedures recommended in the safety compliance software were being ignored or incorrectly followed. This was particularly evident in one of the Latin American operator sites. In many of our interviews it was clear that managers were happy to ascribe poor compliance with systems to the general ineptness or irresponsibility of local operators, or poor installation and maintenance of the system by local support teams. Few were able or willing to take the analysis much further.

Our interviewee had dug much deeper than this, however. As CEO of a company offering safety-critical software on which various oil majors relied, and being an engineer by training, he felt the need to unpick and if necessary reengineer the process that was causing the failure of the system. That system failure turned out to be as much social as technical.

On closer investigation with users, it seemed that standard safety procedures were in fact not standard at all. They fell into two groups:

- the generic ones that relate to immutable laws of physics and human physiology and can be standardized (global);

- those that vary according to local conditions, local cultures of behaviour and local perceptions of what will work in those conditions (local).

As new procedures were rolled out, local staff recognized that some of these procedures either wouldn't work, or were regarded as so inappropriate as to be unworkable, and they were increasingly ignored. In some cases another unofficial and therefore invisible and unmonitored system had replaced the formally supported one. This then established a de facto norm of ignoring standard procedures in general. Thus even the generic safety standards were actually being more frequently breached as a result of the attempt to ensure better safety compliance across sites.

Ironically, standardizing safety procedures was actually increasing risk. This falls into the category of what Peter Senge classes as an archetype, where a failure to see the dynamics of the systemic process can lead to fixes that actually create a vicious circle which is ultimately counter to what is intended.

Two strands have to be aligned here – one technical and one human:

- the need to harness the benefits of standardization and interoperability work across a global information system (*technical interoperability*);
- the need to ensure that standards and procedures work on the ground at the level of local information systems – cognitive, communicative, social, organizational, political, economic or cultural (*semantic, social, organizational and cross-cultural interoperability*).

## Solution

The solution adopted here is a generically applicable one. It is based on standardizing the universals online and on paper (those aspects that are dictated by invariable principles, for example human physiology and the laws of physics), and giving responsibility to locally knowledgeable managers to interpret, specify and enforce the most locally viable interpretation of the requirements.

- Central management now had a better understanding of the local operational context and dynamics.
- Local managers had a clearer role as intermediaries in the process of interfacing the knowledge and the policy gap between central and local management.
- Local users had a functional variant of the procedures.
- System designers had clearer guidelines on what could be locked down and what was likely to vary in the future.

From a safety and a business perspective, there was a reduction in non-compliance or departure from the standard procedures that the company had a remit to ensure for their clients. From a technical perspective, it meant that ongoing changes and adaptations did not require complete

> system redesign (which has time and cost implications) or constant modification (which results in loss of design coherence or flexibility, loss of dependability and knock on effects on system performance in other areas).

# IMPLICATIONS FOR DESIGN AND MANAGEMENT

The main point here is that many standard procedures and assumptions are not standard in other contexts where people, processes and technology relate in different ways, and where the cognitive, social and cultural shapers of behaviour are also different. Some of these differences follow recognized patterns associated with general cultural differences identified in cross-cultural research – as for example in the supply chain cases described in Chapter 4.

Often interviews with local managers or operatives highlighted a range of issues that were common knowledge on the ground, but which were not picked up as part of the kind of strategic analysis and feedback routinely carried out for central management.

Social networks are unique and under-used systems for generating, sharing and implementing knowledge of local environments. They are evolutionary solutions to problems of knowledge management across communities. The examples that follow go beyond simple alignment to active leverage of this resource to create value for all the stakeholders.

## CASE 2: LEVERAGING BACK- AND FRONT-END KNOWLEDGE

### CREATING GLOBAL AND LOCAL VALUE IN WEB-BASED REPOSITORIES

'Modern high speed networks push back-end intelligence and front-end intelligence in two different directions, towards opposite ends of the network. Back-end intelligence becomes embedded into a shared infra-structure at the core of the networks, while front-end intelligence fragments into many forms at the periphery of the network, where the users are. And since value follows intelligence, the two ends of the network become the major sources of potential profits.'

M. SAWHNEY and D. PARIKH, 2001,
'Where value lives in a networked world'

### Problem

For many networked systems, the sheer diversity of stakeholding users represents a barrier to interoperability, as in the case of the previous example of safety compliance software. In some cases this very diversity can also be used to advantage in maintaining the currency and sustainability of shared assets.

## Creating Value from Both Ends of the Network

Both technical and social information systems have the potential to create value. Knowledge-based technology at the back-end can benefit from front-end user knowledge to create, adapt or implement it in different local contexts. Scran Learning Images is a huge digital image archive with thousands of users. Web-based tools allow very diverse and distributed user groups to create local value in very different ways. They are able to use the technical engine to digitize, upload, share, reuse or repurpose elearning resources in locally adaptable ways, including external websites, and also as part of a sustainable shared resource for the networked community as a whole.

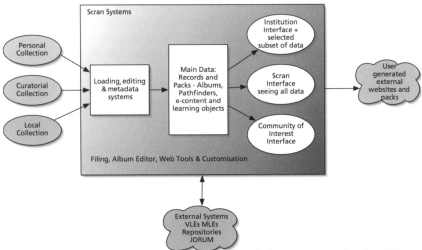

FIGURE 1.1 *Leveraging back- and front-end knowledge to create value for different users*

The environment allows users to leverage the technical resource to their own ends. The platform is an open source sandpit for creative collaboration across sectors or communities in the generation or repurposing of elearning materials from pre-assembled units of text and images, either as a final output, or as the basis for a more individually tailored resources on a proprietary VLE or repository.

Each user group uses the back-end system to digitize, upload, curate and display their images under their own banner and to their own specifications. As with just in time (JIT) production, the user is able to dictate the selection and individualization of the technical resource to meet their own ends, while the archive benefits in many cases from specialist resources created by an expert community of practice.

Value is thus created at both ends of the network, providing a sustainable model for maintaining currency and use of the archive in ways that meet the changing needs of very diverse user groups. Maintaining the coherence of a technical system need not be at odds with the need to respond to changing local requirements. The evolving concept of pliant computing and of co-design is a reflection of this.

As the quote at the start of the chapter suggests, business value can come from the aggregation of distributed local knowledge, and the brokerage of both knowledge assets and business processes that create value. Another example is the approach taken by one of the E-Social Science Pilot Demonstrator Projects supported by the Economics and Social Science Research Council. The 'Grid Fusion of Global Data and Local Knowledge' project aims to improve the effectiveness of decision-making about business policy and local government policy by exploiting the unique strengths of the grid infrastructure to 'establish secure communications between data-holders with market knowledge and scientists experienced in the application of analytical techniques that require a high-performance computing infrastructure'.

The project aims to migrate the process of analysing corporate data from a secure high performance computing (HPC) environment, to a secure grid environment in the Asia-Pacific region to demonstrate model building on real corporate data from global companies, at different levels of aggregation. It leverages back-end technology on a large scale and a range of unique local datasets on customer behaviour from the periphery as the basis for creating value. Grid-based web services have the potential to use huge technical resources to leverage huge datasets of hetero-geneous and distributed information from the bleeding edge, where local knowledge holds the potential for innovation or localization of marketing strategy if it can be meaningfully aggregated and interpreted.

## IMPLICATIONS FOR DESIGN AND MANAGEMENT OF SOCIO-TECHNICAL SYSTEMS

Fire is a complex, dynamic phenomenon in which small differences in initial conditions lead to large differences in outcome. Designing structures to reduce risk of fire in the first place, and to facilitate rapid intervention should it occur, are critical elements in a risk mitigation strategy ... Such a strategy assumes that an engineered building, with its occupants, constitutes a socio-technical system, and that many buildings, with their occupants, create a wider community that can anticipate, reduce, or increase risk.

L. COMFORT, 2002, *'Anticipating fire:*
*A socio-technical approach to mitigation'*

Socio-technical systems have complex dynamics in which small differences in initial conditions lead to large differences in outcomes. This quote highlights the value of a design and management remit that encompasses the social and the technical network as complementary knowledge-based resources requiring synergy. The cases outline different kinds of synergy – between central and local teams, or between systems that operate in mutually reinforcing ways. In two of the cases, a symbiotic arrangement uses the knowledge of two coupled systems to mutual benefit, highlighting the importance of sharing knowledge across communities and across systems. The ebusiness case that follows in the next chapter highlights some of the very recurrent problems associated with sharing and reusing distributed knowledge held by business and the technical teams designing another kind of socio-technical system – large company extranet.

## FURTHER READING

Bijker, W. and Law, J. (eds) (1992) *Shaping Technology, Building Society: Studies in Sociotechnical Change*. MIT Press, Cambridge, MA.

British Computer Society Sociotechnical Group Archive www.sociotechnical.org/London_prev_lect.htm.

Chatwin, B. (1978) *The Songlines*. Picador Edition, Pan Books in association with Jonathan Cape, London.

Coakes, E., Willis, D. and Clarke, S. (eds) (2001) *Knowledge Management in the Sociotechnical World: The Graffiti Continues*. Springer Verlag, London.

Comfort, L. (2002) Anticipating fire: A socio-technical approach to mitigation. *Technology* 7: 33–42.

Giddens, A. (1993) *Sociology*, 2nd edition. Polity, London.

Harris, J. and Henderson, A. (1999) A better mythology of computing, CHI1999, www.pliant.org/talk-7-99.pdf.

Mackenzie, D. (1999) *The Social Shaping of Technology*. Open University Press, Buckingham.

Mumford, E. (1983) Participative systems design: Practice and theory. *Journal of Occupational Behavior* 4: 47–57.

Nonaka, I. and Nishiguchi, T. (eds) (2001) *Knowledge Emergence: Social, Technical and Evolutionary Dimensions of Knowledge Creation*. Oxford University Press, Oxford.

Orlikowski, W. (2000) Using technology and constituting structures: A practice lens for studying technology in organisations. *Organization Science* 11(4).

Pasmore, W. A. (1988) *Designing Effective Organizations: The Sociotechnical Systems Perspective*. Wiley, New York.

Sawhney, M. and Parikh, D. (2001) Where value lives in a networked world. *Harvard Business Review*, January 2001: 175–198.

Trist, E. (1981) The evolution of socio-technical systems. Occasional Paper no. 2. Ontario Quality of Working Life Centre, Toronto.

# 2 Aligning Social and Technical Systems to Create Value

*Why create costs, when you can create value.*

*Anon*

There are many contexts where invisible forces have tangible impacts, which can be mapped and managed by alignment and leverage, by conversion, or by more effective linkage. Often the means by which we achieved this is so familiar we may fail to recognize it as such. Imagine a world without maps for example. Until we agreed on conventions for representing space and distance on paper,[1] individual knowledge was restricted to the shared limits of the visible horizon. The social validation of this simple frame of reference, however, allows the distributed knowledge of the many to be shared and used to facilitate the cost, speed and effectiveness of travel beyond the immediate visual frame of reference.

In initiatives as diverse as business innovation systems, or knowledge discovery systems, there is a growing awareness that the distributed, agent-based architecture of society is a sophisticated information system in itself, with dynamics and regularities that impact (positively or negatively) on technical systems. Cognitive, social and cultural systems are not neutral. The dynamics they generate follow patterns that experienced managers have always recognized and used. The sudden expansion of such systems across multiple regions has to some extent moved practice beyond established wisdom. Patterns have emerged from the evidence of high profile failures, where the extension of regional or national business strategies have failed to generate expected outcomes when exposed to the less familiar risks of the global market.

The concept of harnessing and converting information and energy between systems is age-old. The sail harnessed wind energy to advantage, in much the same way as the web-based ebusinesses increasingly harness the knowledge and behaviour of users, or political enterprises have sought to co-opt religious and commercial ones. The cases suggest two things of relevance to designers and managers:

- the design of such systems has been constrained by technical frames of reference, yet their use in practice is coupled to human ones – whether social, cultural, organizational or political;

- the apparent complexity of socio-technical systems masks a recurring set of archetypes, or generic scenarios, knowledge of which provide the potential to add value and cut cost/risk.

## HOW CAN COUPLED SYSTEMS CREATE VALUE?

Socio-technical systems are coupled systems that can potentially harness the information and knowledge generation potential of both technical and human systems to shared ends. Luis Rocha's 'TalkMine' project was an early example of digital library software designed to do just that in ways that have since been adapted by commercial companies.

Technical systems interoperate by mediating systems called middleware that convert information from one system into a format usable by the other system. Human social systems use metaphors, shared context and shared frames of reference as vehicles for mediating understanding across different groups.

The challenge for distributed systems of human and computer agents is to create a means of drawing on the technical and the human resource to mutual benefit.

## DIGITAL REPOSITORIES

### CASE 3: LEVERAGING THE TECHNICAL AND THE HUMAN RESOURCE

#### THE 'TALKMINE' DIGITAL LIBRARY PROJECT

#### Context

Digital repositories and libraries are traditionally very passive models of networked systems. In addition to the problems of making this accessible for search and retrieval by different user groups, such systems are often unable to adapt to changing requirements, or to benefit from the knowledge of the community of human users. Traditional information retrieval algorithms do not effectively use the implicit knowledge accumulated from usage patterns, or knowledge that users can hold about related domains.

The user community is in itself a knowledge-based system, geared to generating knowledge of the changing environment in which ebusiness systems must compete.

The 'TalkMine' project has built particularly on the potential to leverage coupled systems – the technical retrieval system of a digital library, and the cognitive and collective retrieval systems of a distributed user-base. It leverages the hidden knowledge in the system to push or recommend books in the way that Amazon does, rather than relying passively on users to know what they want in advance. Active recommendation systems based on adaptive environments are both collaborative and content based, because they integrate information from the patterns of usage of groups of users and also categorize database content or semantics in a manner relevant to those groups.

The designers describe this approach as 'open-ended self-organization and adaptation of integrated knowledge networks to (meet) the particular needs of the users of such networks' or more simply, as *Adaptive Webs*. They are applicable to any searchable system, and have already been applied to networks of published documents, websites, networks of felons obtained from intelligence records, and gene networks.

Coupled systems can therefore be designed in ways that create value by supporting system-user learning or evolution. In this case this is used to recombine knowledge in different information resources, to infer new categories of keywords – or to recommend resources that particular user groups have also found relevant in the way that, for example, Amazon does.

# STRATEGIES FOR ALIGNING SOCIAL AND TECHNICAL SYSTEMS

Both system designers and system managers need to cut costs and add value. One of the strategies for adding value is the alignment of technical and human information systems towards more effective generation and management of knowledge – creating value for users and for the system. The two strategies highlighted in this chapter are:

- aligning 'coupled' systems through a web-based interface;
- building technology around a cognitive or a social process.

The following example looks at the value generated by building the technology around the cognitive process of searching for, and making sense of, information, mapping the architecture of the technical system onto the generic architecture of visual and cognitive information systems of human users – essentially building on a common platform that all users have and can use.

## CASE 4: BUILDING TECHNOLOGY AROUND THE COGNITIVE PROCESS

### THE WEBSOM SELF-ORGANIZING MAP

Socio-technical systems build technology around the regularities of cognitive and social structures and processes at those interfaces where information can be exchanged and actions can be generated.

The example below is taken from a digital library of over a million documents, organized around a measure of semantic similarity using keywords. The web-based self-organizing map (WebSOM) is an ordered map of the information space where similar documents lie near each other on the map. The order helps in finding related documents once any interesting document is found.

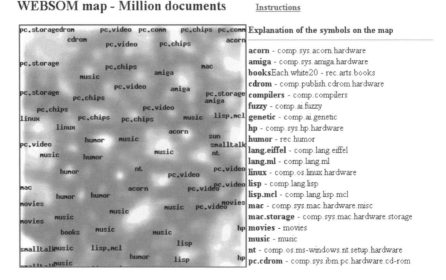

**WEBSOM map - Million documents**    <u>Instructions</u>

Explanation of the symbols on the map

**acorn** - comp.sys.acorn.hardware
**amiga** - comp.sys.amiga.hardware
**books**Each white20 - rec.arts.books
**cdrom** - comp.publish.cdrom.hardware
**compilers** - comp.compilers
**fuzzy** - comp.ai.fuzzy
**genetic** - comp.ai.genetic
**hp** - comp.sys.hp.hardware
**humor** - rec.humor
**lang.eiffel** - comp.lang.eiffel
**lang.ml** - comp.lang.ml
**linux** - comp.os.linux.hardware
**lisp** - comp.lang.lisp
**lisp.mcl** - comp.lang.lisp.mcl
**mac** - comp.sys.mac.hardware.misc
**mac.storage** - comp.sys.mac.hardware.storage
**movies** - movies
**music** - music
**nt** - comp.os.ms-windows.nt.setup.hardware
**pc.cdrom** - comp.sys.ibm.pc.hardware.cd-rom

FIGURE **2.1** *WebSOMs cluster information by a measure of semantic similarity (websom.hut.fi/websom/milliondemo/html/root.html)*

The WebSOM mimics the cognitive architecture of information representation, clustering information in cognate sets, by degree of similarity and difference. It also mimics the architecture of visual information search and retrieval, such as scanning and zooming in from higher order clusters down to sub-clusters, and finally to the individual document to look in more detail.

This conceptual layering from higher-order categories of similar objects, down to sub-categories is also a feature of cognitive organization. From a user-interface perspective, it also facilitates the meaningful presentation of very large datasets in context within the constraints of a small screen. From an information processing perspective, it allows the user to search more efficiently – drawing on contextual cues, and also limiting initial search to a few higher-order categories before attempting to engage with detailed content at a lower level. For human users, with limited cognitive processing capacity, this allows rapid and effective sense-making with large datasets – well beyond what would normally be possible.

The WebSOM map gives a visual overview of thousands of digital library documents contextualized in terms of their similarity or difference based on a measure of semantic correlation. As new digital records are added, this layered map assimilates them, and accommodates the visual record in the same way as cognitive maps are assumed to do.

By building technology around the cognitive and the social process, WebSOMs make it possible for users to understand and act quickly when dealing with datasets that could not be processed by traditional means. In terms of designing for grid computing, for example, size is not the issue – it is sense-making that is important, since value will accrue from the interpretation and implementation of this flood of information.

Agent-based defence systems provide classic examples of socio-technical systems where users need to understand and act quickly when dealing with large and diverse datasets. The speed and accuracy with which agents in the field can make battle decisions is crucial in a very direct sense. The variance in performance in 'distributed agent-based systems' such as this, is increasingly assigned to the different ways in which we select, structure and contextualize information to create meaning and decide on actions.

## CASE 5: BUILDING TECHNOLOGY AROUND THE SOCIAL PROCESS

### THE DIGITAL IMAGE ARCHIVE

Another strategy is based on the win–win principle of strategic alliancing, sharing resources and knowledge to common ends, and thus offering more for less. The web-based tool in the Figure 2.2 allows local users to generate elearning objects from an image archive. These elearning objects are then available to anyone sharing a password on the network (local, regional, national or international, as required).

This provides:

- sustainable production of shareable, reusable community-specific resources;

- a sustainable model for generating, updating and promoting new resources to very distributed and heterogeneous users;

- new opportunities for collaborative networking, resource sharing and collaboration.

The Common Information Environment (CIE) being developed by the Joint Information Systems Committee (JISC) for the UK further and higher education community is a similar concept for sharing and reusing resources at a national level via a common hub. Aligning the aims, resources and systems of stakeholding communities adds competitive advantage, much as strategic alliancing has done in business consortia.

**Click / select images**

**Add / adapt text**

FIGURE 2.2 *Creating reusable, online resources*

## STRATEGIES FOR SENSE-MAKING AND KNOWLEDGE DISCOVERY

The WebSOM in Figure 2.1 highlights our dependence on contextual frames of reference to extract meaning. In this case the system arranges and structures the information in a form that builds on the structure of our own software in cognition and perception. The reverse strategy can also create dividends, facilitating knowledge discovery from the correlation of previously fragmented or distributed information into cognate sets. Two pieces of information, when put together in a context, may create further insights that are not evident from the individual items. A useful analogy here is the jigsaw. Two pieces may have little intrinsic meaning alone. Put together they will increase knowledge of possible other linkages, and eliminate other previously possible ones. They will also provide knowledge of the collective whole being assembled. This information is not resident in any of the pieces as individual elements – only in relation to each other, and to the context of the whole jigsaw picture.

Many databases are never fully leveraged, for this reason, and the following example suggests how providing the right cognate or social lens can bring the meaning suddenly into focus in ways that can facilitate interpretation, action and value.

### From distributed data to situated knowledge: making sense of terrorist communication data

A recent project at the Los Alamos National Laboratory pulled together a range of heterogeneous datasets on the terrorists believed to be involved in the Al Qaeda attack on September 11th. This included mobile phone data and other information on locations and known personal links. The datasets here were large and heterogeneous. Intuitive search by human users is severely constrained. Mathematical analysis may capture significant patterns not otherwise evident but, often, making sense of this data requires organizing it around a familiar situated frame of reference within which we already have operating rules.

Social networks have recently become popular as a means of scaffolding this kind of information in ways that allow sufficient understanding to enhance management of processes such as knowledge sharing or social capital in the organization. In this case, reorganizing diverse datasets around the communication network of the terrorist suspects generated validation of known links in a graphically comprehensible way. This also suggested likely relationships where current knowledge was not available and probable ones that could be investigated, but would not otherwise have been recognized as significant. In other words, knowledge of the social context allowed the analysts to make sense of the information. Getting information is not the problem, so much as making sense of it.

## IMPLICATIONS FOR DESIGN AND MANAGEMENT OF SOCIO-TECHNICAL SYSTEMS

All the information in these cases was available from the outset, but not in a form that was evident to the users. Knowledge and value derived from the way it was extracted and mapped onto a frame of reference users could act on. Understanding and action are situated and the problem with many networked systems is not the scale of the data so much as the difficulty of making sense of it in ways which are of value to users, in this case in the way it was structured, or represented.

The technical architecture in the TalkMine example (see Chapter 1) was designed to map onto the existing cognitive architecture of human users. By building on what is a common platform a degree of interoperability is achieved, together with a degree of intuitive usability that adds value and cuts costs. This is a classic means of leveraging the human and the technical resources to advantage, and the most striking examples have been developed in areas such as defence and ebusiness. These are both volatile environments, where large, diverse information sets have to be represented, shared, interpreted and actioned by distributed agents, and where speed, cost and accuracy are often at a premium.

One of the difficulties is the perception of networked systems as somehow independent of their users after the initial requirements analysis phase. The constant addition and updating of user requirements is often seen as a problem rather than an opportunity for leveraging the technical and the human resource.

## NOTES

1. The aboriginal 'songlines' represent a similar concept, shared in song and ritual enactment rather than on paper, with each tribe preserving the knowledge

of their particular bit of historical time and geographical space, as part of a larger Australian whole (Chatwin, 1998).

## FURTHER READING

Burt, R. S. (2001) Structural holes versus network closure as social capital. In Lin, N., Cook, K. and Burt, R. S. (eds) *Social Capital. Theory and Research*. Walter, New York.

Bush, V. (1945) As we may think. *Atlantic Monthly* 176 (July): 101–108.

Galeghar, J., Kraut, R. E. and Egido, C. (eds) (1990) *Intellectual Teamwork: Social and Technological Foundations of Cooperative Work*. Lawrence Erlbaum, Hillsdale, NJ.

Honkelaa, T., Kaski, S., Kohonen, T. and Lagus, K. (1998) Self-organizing maps of very large document collections: Justification for the WEBSOM method. In Balderjahn, I., Mathar, R. and Schader, M. (eds) *Classification, Data Analysis, and Data Highways*. Springer, Berlin. websom.hut.fi/websom/.

Rocha, L. and Bollen, J. (2001) Biologically motivated distributed design. In Segel, L. and Cohen, I. (eds) *Design Principles for the Immune Systems and Other Distributed Autonomous Systems*. Santa Fe Institute Studies in the Sciences of Complexity. Oxford University Press, Oxford.

Shneiderman, B. (1997) *Designing the User Interface: Strategies for Effective Human-Computer Interaction*. Addison-Wesley, Harlow.

# 3 Aligning Knowledge and Objectives in Enterprise Systems

*Interviewer:*
*You've mentioned the problem of changes late in the design of the system. Can you think of anything that might have helped avoid this?*
*Technical Manager:*
*A cluster bomb perhaps?*

## PORTALS: eBUSINESS

The development of extended enterprise systems, migrating and extending the business process to web-based systems, is acknowledged to be a high-cost, high-risk process that has its own raft of problem scenarios. A surprising recurring feature of interviews with technical managers is the non-technical nature of the most obstinate and costly problems. The technical issues are often hijacked by human ones at every level: cognitive, social, cultural, organizational, economic and political.

### Context

Extended enterprise systems are unrivalled socio-technical systems and depend on the integrated management of knowledge within a broad spectrum of organizational transactions between people, processes and technology. Effective design and management of such systems implies an understanding of the individual elements, their interdependencies and the means by which they combine to create value where appropriately managed. The same elements, however, can cause crucial gaps, ambiguities and contradictions that have cost implications for an organization. The example below is useful in highlighting:

- a range of recurring problem scenarios of a socio-technical and socio-political nature;
- the difficulty of sharing knowledge across different communities;
- the difficulty of aligning the aims and criteria of different stakeholder groups.

The third point is one that is often underestimated in knowledge management discussions, but one that frequently overrides other factors.

## CASE 6: KNOWLEDGE SHARING IN SYSTEM DESIGN

### THE eBUSINESS EXTRANET

### Problem

This large financial services company aimed to make their system more accessible to customers and to third-party intermediaries to allow, for example, the facility to offer rapid quotes online in selling their (very complex) financial packages. They decided it would be useful to document the most recurrent problems encountered in the process, with some of the principal strategies that had been developed to deal with them. These were problems we recognized in many different companies where the design process had been a painful one, and one where a recurring collection of socio-technical problems and strategies were evident. The initial problems often stemmed from the difficulty of aligning the knowledge and aims of very different stakeholding communities:

- Aligning distributed knowledge in a shared frame of reference: A business manager has knowledge of the business requirements rather than the technical constraints. A technical manager has knowledge of the technical requirements and may not understand the full implications of a complex business such as finance, in a moving market.

- Aligning aims, criteria and rewards: A business manager will be rewarded for meeting customers' needs faster and better than the competition. A technical manager is more likely to be rewarded by his peers for a coherent and robust design, on schedule and within budget.

- Aligning views on proposed courses of action: A business and a technical manager may have different preferred technical solutions to meet the business requirements, and these will involve trade-offs and compromises whose implications will not necessarily be immediately obvious at the outset. Figure 3.1 shows the tensions at play in the system design process.

In the initial phase the problem was a classic case of the difficulty of knowledge sharing across domains heightened by the scale of the operation, the diversity of different stakeholding partners, the volatility of the market, and the sheer complexity of the product to non-specialists. The problems that arose were recognized by managers involved in the design of systems in many other organizations.

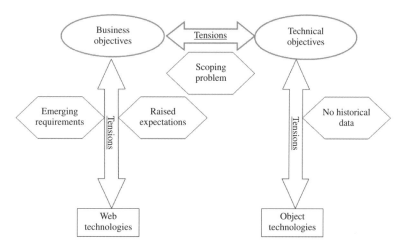

**FIGURE 3.1** *Tensions in system design*

## Aligning knowledge

TABLE 3.1 *Aligning knowledge*

| Phase 1 Aligning knowledge | |
| --- | --- |
| Recurring problem | Solution |
| Knowledge transfer across domains requires a shared space, a shared language and shared aims. However, distributed departments do not have informal social opportunities to develop this. | Co-location of project team representing different stakeholder groups.<br><br>Shared space online as well as onsite to support knowledge building through dialogue and shared experience. |
| Knowledge assets are not available as there is no historical data of expertise on recurring problem-solution pairs. | Create a knowledge-base of recurring problem–solution cases that are socio-technical, and use agreed terms. |
| Knowledge is withheld or manipulated by different stakeholders. | Co-located project teams identify what they don't know that might alter the nature and sequence of project planning.* |
| Narrow view of required knowledge. | |
| Difficulty in understanding the full requirements and implications of complex business processes. | Maintain a core team which has developed (a) expertise and credibility across its members' areas of expertise, and (b) shared frames and terms of reference. |

\* This was identified as central in collaborative project planning in oil and gas drilling systems, for example. Here time was at a premium, and knowledge of interdependent activities provided opportunities for cutting costs significantly by reengineering over a shorter period. (We are indebted to Phil Murray of Petrotechnics for this example.)

Typically, scoping the task was a problem that was understood very differently by the business and technical communities collaborating on the system. Technologists were keen to identify requirements early and create a robust and coherent system on time, and within budget. Business managers, on the other hand, had very different priorities. They were keen to ensure that emerging requirements were addressed even if this was late in the design of the system, with associated costs and design complications. In the design of future systems, it was clearly of value for the company to preserve and augment the knowledge of a range of problems: solution scenarios as a means of cutting cost and risk, as well as providing new staff with a resource based on core company knowledge.

There is clearly a demand for cases that would allow companies to build on successful solutions, and clever win–win scenarios are possible. In most scenarios, however, technical choices must be made which trade off costs and benefits. In such a context, a range of possibilities is informative. Each solution will have pros and cons which benefit some groups over others; the choice will ultimately be as much about power relations between communities, as about knowledge of possible options. Few people with experience of organizational decision-making will have failed to recognize the role of formal and informal networks, and the value of social capital. Some of the more interesting models of socio-technical systems draw on structuration theory and enactment theory as a means of understanding these dynamics.

It was clear from several cases that a project team drawn from different disciplines also needed to be physically co-located wherever possible. This provided a shared space that is difficult to recreate in distributed contexts. The natural dynamics of social exchange support the development of shared frames of reference, a jointly agreed modus operandi and the reinforcement of behaviour that supports collective project ends rather than the individual ends of departments, domains or individuals. The checks and balances of social interaction are inherent shapers of collective behaviour, generating the invisible structures we call society. Trust acts like an authentication system in accessing the power of a social network. Rewards contingent on particular behaviours shape collective actions in particular ways. Power allocates rewards to reinforce desired behaviours. This area is one of the most interesting from a design and a management perspective. Although it is about aligning the knowledge of social/organizational/professional communities to a common end, the means by which technology can extend or enhance the cognitive and social infrastructure is still emerging. Different perspectives on this are pulled together in the final chapter of the book.

## *Aligning objectives*

TABLE 3.2 *Aligning objectives*

| Phase 2 Aligning objectives | |
| --- | --- |
| Recurring problem | Solution |
| Competing aims and requirements. | Ensure a detailed business plan is in place, with criteria agreed and enforced, before embarking on the technical design. |
| Constantly emerging requirements (creep) leading to additional costs, risks and delays as a design is repeatedly revised or added to. Late changes are particularly costly and impact greatly on other design aspects. | Separate core invariant elements from peripheral and variable elements where possible, to limit the cost and scale of redesign while allowing flexibility to meet the market requirements. |
| An initial solution of matching requirements with set criteria of costs and benefits is often overridden by lobby groups in the senior management team who 'move the goal posts' and undermine the official change control processes. | |
| Early mock-ups and prototypes make stakeholders more aware of the real implications, risks and opportunities of a new system, leading to changes in priorities and requirements at a late stage of the build. | |
| Getting support from management for invisible or long-term initiatives which may have implications for future competitiveness. | Show the benefits and risks with other company examples.<br><br>Share resources with other groups with shared concerns. |

In this stage, lack of understanding was compounded by the different priorities and criteria of different groups. It was clear from discussion with technical staff that success was defined (and rewarded) within this domain by a system that was on time, on budget, and with a robust and coherent design.

This was not a view shared by the various business factions, whose main concern was not cost, not time and not the robustness of the design. Their main priority was, understandably, to ensure that they would be able to maintain, or possibly even enhance their ability to meet customers' needs on the new system. Roles, rewards, objectives and power relations clearly impacted on this stage of the project. As initial mock ups were developed, and users became more aware of how the system would impact on their activities, they became aware of new issues and complications they wished resolved, and began to see the potential for building in additional functionality. This is an unavoidable problem in a volatile business environment.

Most design problems in socio-technical systems are what can be termed wicked problems, where there are:

- continuously emerging requirements or requirement creep;

- moving goalposts – stakeholders' view of the project develops and conceptual or political positions change in unpredictable ways;

- unknown (often unknowable) aspects of system use in dynamic environments.

As a result, requirements, priorities and associated design solutions are constantly in need of revision. Constraints on time and budget are exceeded as designers attempt to achieve a coherent and robust design despite constant adjustments and restarts. The solution is never complete. The solution has often been to act as if these were tame problems and adhere to the more quantifiable and familiar technical requirements, and minimize the impact of a range of emerging non-technical requirements. In this case, the creep in ongoing requirements led to a situation where the aims and criteria of those building the system were directly at odds with those of the users. Late design changes threaten the robustness of a well-designed system, and may mean a complete redesign from first principles. This may result in extra cost, and delay in completion and rollout.

At this point different groups started lobbying for their particular requirements, or for their particular preferred design solution, or to reconsider the criteria for adopting particular approaches previously set by the technical designers. The political architecture of the organization then determined the crucial interfaces and the final choice of design solution in disputed instances. This stage was a stressful one for all concerned, involving compromise in terms of both design and require-ments, with substantial delays and higher costs than originally budgeted for. Everyone recognizes this scenario and the potential cost of failing to manage it, yet it is rarely planned for.

The design of the portal software around the business process required that:

 (i) the business process was fully agreed in advance;
 (ii) the criteria (or the arbiters) for design choices were defined in advance;
(iii) the process of identifying, validating and implementing those choices was honoured.

A surprising number of the negative scenarios encountered were generic, yet most managers were unaware that other companies had faced similar issues, and were reassured that this was so. The lack of a platform for sharing such examples, and the human and the financial cost savings implicit in this, underpinned the decision to attempt to document some of these experiences, (know what) and document the expertise associated with particular individual (know who). While much of the experience and expertise was hard to document on paper, the process of attempting to do so was a valuable opportunity to develop some shared reference points as a basis for collaborative working, and the mapping of expertise held by individuals allowed for collaborative reconstruction of the relevant aspects in future eventualities

## *Aligning expectations*

TABLE 3.3 *Aligning Expectations*

| Phase 3 Aligning expectations | |
|---|---|
| Recurring problem | Solution |
| Hyped anticipation of outcome. | Under-promise and over-deliver design, and roll out discrete chunks, so human and technical challenges are more manageable. |
| Cost and development time of prototype, followed by changes to spec. | Collaborative prototyping of rapidly generated mock-up. |
| Capturing knowledge of solutions to recurring problems. | Matrix of organizational expertise. |

Having designed the system, more problems were still to follow. Typically, the design of a new web-based system is oversold at the outset, partly to generate buy-in from management. The first rollout of a system to a very diverse audience, with high individual expectations, is often disappointment, compounded with the annoyance of working with the inevitable initial bugs in a new system.

Rolling out such an extensive new system necessarily highlighted multiple minor problems simultaneously. The team were fire fighting on several fronts. Their experience, and the experience of many managers has been to do one of two things on subsequent projects. For example, if it is possible, break up the project into chunks that can be rolled out separately and better managed around the needs of particular groups. If, as often is the case, the project cannot be broken up, they aim to under-promise and over-deliver. This operates on the principle that you promise something fairly straightforward and produce more than specified. This way, the resulting offering is perceived as better than anticipated, despite the inevitable bugs and interruptions of normal processes.

# IMPLICATIONS FOR DESIGN AND MANAGEMENT OF SOCIO-TECHNICAL SYSTEMS

As with most systems covered in the course of a range of separate projects, the problems were not so much technical, as socio-technical and socio-political.

Requirements are often emergent and contingent – they change during the process itself. As system designers have had cause to note, the very act of providing a first prototype is enough for users to see the whole system in a new light and add further new or contradictory requirements that threaten the project as a whole. So-called wicked problems arise from the fluid and evolving nature of open systems such as business enterprises operating in evolving markets. Every solution is one shot. Attempting to solve wicked problems changes the problem space – you never get a second shot. As earlier cases showed, these can generate a never-ending loop of requirements creep that has a knock on effect on the costs, the time to completion, the coherence and the robustness of a system that is constantly modified. Although this example only covers the issues that were brought up in interview, they were also typical of many other conversations with managers of very different systems.

# THE DIFFICULTY OF ALIGNING CONSTRUCTS AND MODELS

As the design of extended enterprise systems distributes knowledge between diverse communities there is a strong argument for understanding the architecture and grammar of knowledge transfer in social as well as technical networks. It would be hard to understand a football match without knowledge of the spatial frame of reference (lines, goals, touchlines, number of players etc) and of the process 'grammar' (order of play, length of first and second half, permissible moves, penalties etc). Equally, knowledge sharing depends on rules and norms, which are socially constructed and enacted in ways that are known to the participants, but may not be clear to outside observers.

Mental models and metaphors that relate to our generic experiences of the world, particularly our physical and sensory experiences, are society's solution to the difficulty of sharing knowledge with groups from other domains. We use it as a kind of inter-language to establishing a shared frame of reference to understand what is brought to the table by different parties.

A file created by another program is either completely or partially unreadable. Similar analogies come from natural information systems such as biology or immunology, where the same biochemical information is understood differently by different organisms. Managers are rapidly becoming aware that human systems are also mediated in this way, with the unfortunate complication that the software from which the knowledge originates varies from community to community and is not easily accessible to inspection. The information itself does not therefore constitute the message. It requires the program or context in which it was created if it is to be accurately interpreted in actionable ways. Without a shared context for what different stakeholder communities know, the organization cannot really 'know what it knows' in the collective sense.

### Creating collective frames of reference

In virtual or distributed communities, shared contexts may have to be explicitly created for dispersed teams. There is a need for:

- shared spaces in which distributed teams can interact;
- shared frames of reference such as mental models, metaphors or problem scenarios in which to define the context of both understanding and decision-making.

In the example above, workshops were provided to give the shared space within the organization where stakeholders from different communities could come together.

### Using time and sequence as an organizing framework

The simplest frame of reference we use to integrate distributed knowledge is the timeline (or the timetable). This is relevant not only to an understanding of when and where particular problems could be anticipated in a future project, but also where actions are required and decisions made. It is worth stressing the view of knowledge as situated understanding and action (see Chapter 6). It is through action that the value of knowledge is unlocked, and action is always located in time and space.

Sequence, cost and speed of events are key criteria for success in most projects, and problem scenarios are often mapped and managed in relation to it, much as project tasks are organized in chronological order in project management software. The timeline as a frame of reference reflects the unifying need to map shared knowledge as a means of cutting project development time.

### Using the organization as a frame of reference

The central configuring metaphor for situating decision-making and action with users often seems to be the organization in which the team is situated and where team members share a social context with a defined set of roles and rules for action such as:

- a conceptual frame of reference for collective understanding in context; and
- a contextual frame of reference for decision-making.

Clearly, other professional environments might be situated in other contexts representing defining roles, relations and transactions. In the case of this particular business organization, recurring design and management problems tended to cluster in ways which reflected the organizational structure itself. Creating a virtual space in which the participants have roles seems a necessary requirement for the kind of social and intellectual engagement of real actors in real contexts.

TABLE 3.4 *Situating recurring socio-technical problems within the context of the organization*

| Organizational level | Type of problem scenario |
| --- | --- |
| Senior/strategic management | At senior management level there was an awareness of people issues impacting on the effectiveness of ebusiness operations that had originally been conceived as largely technical challenges. |
| Operational/middle management | Most socio-technical issues that were cited arose at the level of middle management where general strategies were translated into practice. This typically related to the alignment of knowledge and aims across stake-holding communities, e.g. trading off technical and financial requirements such as cost against emerging business ones. |
| Technical implementation | Technical implementation obviously has human factor issues, but these were not cited as serious socio-technical issues that impacted on the success of the project. |

One of the biggest challenges to the design and management of collaborative, networked systems on a global scale, such as supply chains or grid-based web services, is the difficulty of sharing knowledge in a dynamic environment, across diverse communities without a shared social or cultural context that supports mutual meanings or situated actions. In social networks, the generation of shared foundations is natural to us; however, even these evolutionary solutions are limited by cultural and linguistic boundaries.

## Aligning aims as well as knowledge

It is worth noting that the problems encapsulated in these patterns are not only associated with the difficulty of aligning knowledge across sites and across sectors. They are also related to the difficulty of aligning competing aims, or criteria, and are most evident at the decision-making stage. These issues are as likely to shape decision-making and outcomes as the sharing of relevant knowledge; for example, the criteria and aims of a design community may be for a robust and elegant design with minimal delay and complication, while the priority for the business community is to optimize its own ability to respond to changing business opportunities and requirements as they emerge, without being constrained by technical considerations.

### Using the problem itself as a frame of reference

The problem definition itself may allow the individual or team to identify the key dimensions or forces which characterize it. These then provide a basis for both identifying relevant knowledge and for organizing it. Cognitive psychology suggests that we organize information in terms of similarity and difference, using salient dimensions to create higher order concepts and categories. This has huge advantages in terms of information processing: it provides us with contextual and associational meaning and reduces cognitive load. This is one reason why concept maps, for example, allow us to make sense of large datasets much more effectively than tables of raw data.

> ### CASE 7: USING THE PROBLEM AS A FRAME OF REFERENCE
>
> #### CAPACITY PLANNING
>
> The following table (Table 3.5) provides an example of a capacity-planning problem identified in a large American real estate company operating in the very volatile ebusiness market.
>
> Defining the problem collectively is arguably central to the process because it is only then that distributed pieces of information, knowledge or experience can be drawn together meaningfully around the salient dimensions. Case-based reasoning, problem-based learning, scenarios and patterns are among a long list of strategies to gaining a common understanding between individuals and across organizations.
>
> The problem is broken down into a set of key dimensions, each with an associated solution. Having a range of solutions, each with different pros and cons, is a useful way of reflecting on the options available. If the deep structure of the problem is made explicit in this way, it is possible to see how new technological options might create new solutions.

## IMPLICATIONS FOR DESIGN AND MANAGEMENT OF KNOWLEDGE-BASED SYSTEMS

The uptake and use of even more extended networked systems such as grid-based web services will be influenced by the extent to which the scale of emerging knowledge from dispersed communities can be used to support sense-making or to advance collective decision-making. Access to larger quantities of diverse sources of data, information and knowledge

TABLE 3.5 *The conceptual relationship of various solutions to a core problem in system design (over-capacity)*

| Context | Problem | Competing requirements | Solutions |
|---|---|---|---|
| Volatility of a more distributed and increasingly user-led market in the extended enterprise makes resource planning and management difficult to forecast and manage effectively. | How can business respond rapidly and effectively to transient user requirements without costs and risks inherent in over- or under-build? | Maximize response to changing scale and scope of user requirements. Minimize cost of system build and/ or redesign. | 1a. Share resources. 1b. Share resources dynamically. 1c. Target resources. |
| | Over capacity is costly and invokes other costs/risks such as security. Under capacity can lead to loss of business due to poor service or system failure. | Maintain reliability, security, flexibility of service. | 1d. Outsource transient capacity. 1e. Align short-term build with long-term planning. |

taken out of context is highlighting the difficulty of knowledge sharing and sense-making across communities with different aims and frames of reference.

# FURTHER READING

Ackerman, M., Volmar, P., and Volker, W. (2003) *Sharing Expertise: Beyond Knowledge Management.* MIT Press, Cambridge, MA.

Cañas, A. J., Carvalho, M. (2004) Concept Maps and AI: An Unlikely Marriage? Proceedings of SBIE 2004: *Simpósio Brasileiro de Informática na Educação,* Manaus, Brazil, 09–12 November. www.ihmc.us/users/acanas/Publications/ConceptMapsAI/Canas-CmapsAI-Sbie2004.pdf.

Checkland, P. and Scholes, J. (1990) *Soft Systems Methodology in Action.* Wiley, Chichester.

Davenport, T. H. and Probst, J. B. (2002) *Knowledge Management Case Book: Siemens Best Practices.* Wiley, Chichester.

Liu, L. and Yu, E. (2003) Designing information systems in social context: A goal and scenario modelling approach. *Information Systems Journal* 29 (2).

Pask, G. (1975) *Conversation, Cognition and Learning: A Cybernetic Theory and Methodology.* Elsevier, Amsterdam.

Pooley, R. and Stevens, P. (1999) *Using UML.* Addison-Wesley, Harlow.

Rosenhead, J., and Mingers, J. (eds) (2001) *Rational Analysis for a Problematic World Revisited: Problem Structuring Methods for Complexity, Uncertainty And Conflict.* Wiley, Chichester.

Ure, J. (2003) Aligning People, Processes and Technology. In Jardim-Goncalves, R., Roy, R., and Steiger-Garcao, A. (eds) *Advances in Concurrent Engineering: Research and Applications.* A. A. Balkema, Swets and Zeitlinger, Lisse.

Von Krogh, F. G., Nonaka, I. and Nishiguchi, T. (2000) *Knowledge Creation.* Macmillan, London.

Weick, K. E. (1995) *Sensemaking in Organizations.* Sage, Thousand Oaks, CA.

Wenger, E. and Snyder, W. (2002) Communities of practice: The organizational frontier. *Harvard Business Review* January/February: 139–145.

# 4 Cross-cultural Architecture in the Automotive Supply Chain

*JIT (Just In Time) procurement works in Germany. Why doesn't it work in Brazil? It's the same technology, so what's the difference?*

*Senior Manager, automotive manufacturing supply chain*

The cases below are taken from a field study carried out in the automotive industry in Brazil. They reveal some of the ways in which local realities can have an impact on the extended enterprise. The application of so-called global business concepts in different local cultural/social environments highlights the fact that business concepts have their own cultural roots and must be aligned with (or adapted to) the local social and cultural realities on the ground, both in terms of the concepts themselves and the nature of local management styles. These examples illustrate critical problem interfaces between people, processes and technologies that become evident when integrating business systems across communities with very diverse geographical, conceptual and cultural mappings of space and time.

Constructs of space and time are central to lean management systems that minimize time and use of space in the production process and management style. These cases demonstrate how even small variations in our internal or collective understanding of time and space, and the relative priorities which we assign to them, can impact on performance at several levels. In many contexts these differences were explained away as a general lack of competence or responsibility, but a misunderstanding of conditions and traditions can make certain problem scenarios highly likely. As companies increasingly extend across underdeveloped regions to achieve lower labour costs, these circumstances are more and more relevant to managers as well as system designers.

## ALIGNING PEOPLE, PROCESSES AND TECHNOLOGY IN A MODULAR CONSORTIUM

The first example is taken from one of the first-tier automotive suppliers in a modular consortium. Figure 4.1 gives a very simplified view of the architecture of the production lines used in this type of manufacturing.

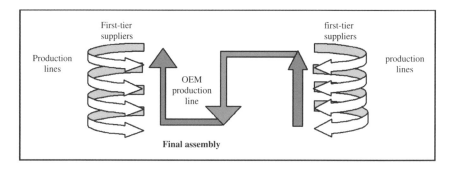

FIGURE 4.1 *Diagram of an OEM's production line with integrated first-tier suppliers' production lines*

In a modular consortium all first-tier suppliers are integrated into the central production process and are located under the same roof as the original equipment manufacturer (OEM). They assemble the modular elements of the product (a car, in this example) on their own production lines. These feed into the manufacturer's production line in such a way that each element is provided *just in time* (JIT) and *just in sequence* (JIS), where and when it is needed. This concept has the advantage of minimizing storage space (which reduces current asset, logistic and warehousing costs) and transport time (required to move modular elements between parts of the production lines).

Only a few hours' supply is ever stocked in an open warehouse system near the suppliers' production lines, and second-tier suppliers must be sited very close (at most 12–15 km away) to the modular consortium to guarantee a supply that is synchronized with production. Warehousing space is calculated on the basis of how long delivery takes.

A modular consortium is therefore designed to save:

- time (through the integration of activities in an optimal sequence and the minimization of distances for transporting parts);

- space (through the local storage for a few hours of only the parts required).

For this vision of synergy to be realized, all these interdependent processes must be flawlessly orchestrated. There is little, if any, margin for error, so failure of one supplier to keep up with the tempo of the main production line generates costly disruption across the whole system. Where it operates successfully, the modular consortium generates enormous production capacities: in this example 250,000 vehicles annually (or one car leaving the production line every 80 seconds).

## Context and problem: Different concepts of space and time

In global markets, high-technology plants are often, perhaps even typically, implemented in underdeveloped rural areas where high subsidies are granted, labour is cheap and space is not at a premium. This is also the case with the modular consortium in the example. It has been set up in an agricultural region with a tropical climate in Brazil. The rhythm of life in these rural community cultures is in stark contrast to that of the highly industrialized countries where the modular consortium was originally developed. This region is typical of many underdeveloped regions being characterized by:

- a poor transport infrastructure (insufficient to guarantee a supply that is synchronous with production) with second-tier suppliers 2000 km away;

- an inadequately skilled labour-force (low levels of basic education) with concepts of space and time shaped by the demands of a rural agricultural economy rather than an industrial one.

Here, space seems an almost unlimited resource (and so is cheap) and time is measured in seasons rather than in vital seconds. In this case, the warehouse space (sufficient for three production days) had been extended/adapted to accommodate the realities of the locality, but there is still a significant risk that the continuous flow of supply could be interrupted (e.g. due to road conditions) and the alternative of air delivery would increase costs dramatically. Figure 4.2 shows the cross-cultural forces to be aligned.

<table>
<tr><td>

***Cultures with restricted space***

- Space is scarce
- Space is expensive
- Order and arrangement are important to save space

</td><td>

</td><td>

***Cultures with unrestricted space***

- Space seems to be unlimited
- Space is cheap
- Order and arrangement are of lesser importance and play a minor role in costs

</td></tr>
</table>

FIGURE 4.2 *Incompatibility of different concepts of space and time*

Harmonizing the differences between these parallel worlds is central to cost-effectiveness, and there are key interfaces where misalignments can disrupt the socio-technical interface.

## CASE 8: IDENTIFYING DIFFERENT CONCEPTS OF SPACE AND TIME

### FIFO SYSTEM AND WAREHOUSING

This case deals with an inventory-based method of warehousing used by a first-tier supplier. As a result of the restricted warehouse space, random storage is used, which means that newly delivered articles will be stored wherever there is space available, enabling better utilization of storage capacity. The supplier combines random storage with the FIFO (first in, first out) inventory evaluation system. This method requires that the stock that is delivered first should be used first. In this case the process is mediated by the FIFO board.

To ensure that the first items in are, in fact, the first items taken out for use, the stock must be accurately registered and the time of delivery must be clearly indicated. By accurate management of time of arrival and location of storage, the parts can be rapidly and accurately retrieved for delivery to the production line. If the associated rules are correctly observed, the FIFO system is an ideal tool that minimizes the use of warehouse space and speedily supplies the production line.

In this case, one employee was responsible for supplying parts to the production line. He functioned as the human interface between the system for allocating space in the warehouse and the system for ensuring the sequence and timing of delivery of parts to the production line. The individual was both observed and interviewed during his daily work. He had difficulty in understanding that following the rules of the FIFO system was a prerequisite for the functioning of the whole system. Consequently, the process was subject to delays and errors. Parts were missing or wrongly allocated on a regular basis, thus hindering the rhythm of production. Frantic attempts often had to be made by other workers to keep feeding the assembly line by searching for missing materials. This confusion also generated further errors at the level of the inventory process, which was by now based on incorrect indications of what was in stock and what needed to be ordered.

This example is one of many similar observations seen across the system. At first glance the response might simply be to assign this to incompetence at the level of staff or local management rather than an intrinsic flaw in the technical or the business concept. Yet the pattern of failure from unpredicted implementation or production problems in many of these cases was consistently linked to the aggregation of such apparently minor deviations by human agents at different levels. When the UK Ministry of Defence invested in a new procurement system used in the Iraq wars, the problems with distribution of supplies was deemed not to be a function of the technical design. The problem arose where the technical system interfaced with the human one. It is here – in the no-man's land between technical and human system design and management that problems typically arose.

## The need to align people, processes and technology

In our main case, the rules imposed on the Brazilian producers were seen by many local staff as unnecessary requirements to work a stupid system imposed from elsewhere. Non-compliance with the rules was often interpreted by the German managers as the incompetence, unreliability or laid-back attitude of the local workforce.

As well as the cultural and conceptual shapers of behaviour, it is worth pointing out that often there are very practical reasons for poor performance. The mechanics of what was actually happening on the ground was rarely accurately investigated or communicated. Instructions, for example, were sometimes provided in German (or English) for Brazilian operators, with obvious potential for error. Both sides tacitly assumed incompetence in the other and the situation remained until highlighted by a German research student on a placement to investigate problems in that particular part of the supply chain.

# ALIGNING PEOPLE, PROCESSES AND TECHNOLOGY IN THE SUPPLY CHAIN

## CASE 9: ALIGNING GLOBAL PROCESSES AND LOCAL PRACTICES

### STANDARD PROCUREMENT AND LOCAL PRACTICES

#### Context

In the automotive sector, as in many other industry sectors (including the computer sector), a platform strategy is adopted. The platform (in this case, a vehicle chassis) is used for different types of car in locations worldwide to cut the cost of parts and standardize on production and processes. The platform accounts for up to 60 percent of the cost of car manufacture. As a result, client satisfaction is achieved through competitive pricing (platform standardization) and variation in design (different models). The flexibility offered by this approach is countered by the risk incurred if the process fails. It is clear from this that extended enterprises employing platform strategy need to be managed and controlled as a flexible system of networked process chains. In terms of procurement of parts/components, central strategies are applied to realize economies of scale: to manage capacity, car manufacturers use a set procedure for ordering parts. This standardized procedure requires both a strict adherence to a sequence of steps and a timeline.

This example deals with the overseas supply chain of a German car manufacturer with regional subsidiaries operating independently in the Latin American market, each with its own central management teams and production locations.

A Latin American logistics department coordinates processes between the regional manufacturing plants. The team is also responsible for information and material flow between Germany and Latin America. The overall purpose is to anticipate problems (taking account of production and delivery times) to avoid the costs of halting the production lines. If for some reason it is not possible to anticipate and order parts sufficiently in advance, there is a risk production will be stopped. Managers have a number of procurement strategies that allow them to trade off the cost of production delays against the cost of alternative means of acquiring parts rapidly.

The procedure for procurement prescribed by the German parent company is based on a very strict regulation of tasks over time. The saying 'one thing at a time' captures the German attitude towards linear (consecutive) time planning where time is compartmentalized according to different tasks.

Working effectively in such a system requires:

- strict adherence to the sequence of steps in the process chain;
- long-term planning and prioritization;
- an understanding of the whole chain of events and their short- and long-term implications for costs, speed, quality assurance and so on, if the sequence is altered.

As indicated earlier, employees in this part of Brazil where the Latin American manufacturing was carried out are also deeply rooted in local culture. Here social networks are powerful resources for solving problems. Attitudes to work are often typified by:

- lack of urgency and forward planning;
- solutions that are socially reached rather than by organizational procedures;
- short-term rather than long-term planning;
- flexible rather than rigid procedures;
- doing things in parallel rather than in sequence.

The networked process chains designed by the German management team reflect their origins in German organizational structures and approaches, which suit the JIT principles. However, as discussed earlier, these concepts are at times counter-productive in an agrarian society and particularly in Brazil, where fluid and undefined situations are a fact of life. In such contexts:

- long-term planning can be almost pointless and planned actions often fail to be realized in practice: laws, rules, deadlines tend to be interpreted as a general guide to action rather than an essential component of them (the spirit, rather than the letter, of the law);
- social processes are more permanent and less volatile than organizational ones, and are therefore accorded greater priority in choosing solutions.

The procurement mismatch between the German and Brazilian cultures is summarized in the following table.

TABLE 4.1 *Invisible architecture: The impact of cultural dynamics on standard business processes*

| Cultural preference | Germany | Brazil |
|---|---|---|
| Avoidance of undefined situations | High | Low |
| Approach to time planning | Long-term, prescriptive | Short-term, flexible |
| Predominating concept of time | Linear, sequential | Synchronous, parallel |
| Approach to rules and regulations | Rigid – the letter of the law | Flexible – the spirit rather than the letter |

An awareness of these differences can provide a basis for choosing (or avoiding) particular combinations of people, processes and technologies to optimize compatibility, create synergies and minimize conflicts.

Even in such complex, dynamic systems, there are recurring patterns that can be recognized and used to avoid unnecessary cost and risk.

## The problem

A sudden and unforeseen increase in demand for a particular car model required the Latin American central logistics department to alter its production schedule. The plan was sent to the Brazilian manufacturing plant with plenty of time for the staff to identify and order all the parts needed for the cars' construction. However, one component needed to be bought from Germany with associated long delivery times. The order was placed too late for delivery to be made in time for production, in spite of the German procedures giving the procurement schedule in great detail. The only solution available to the plant was to change the production schedule and suffer the associated costs and loss of image incurred.

## The need to align people, processes and technology

Platform strategy and global sourcing are intended to reduce costs and create value. However, cultural forces driving organizational and social behaviour are very often at odds and may act to actually increase costs rather than create value, as seen in this case. Companies must therefore balance cost reduction strategies associated with global standardization against the risk of the system becoming dysfunctional through cultural misalignment.

Further investigation of the reasons for the late procurement of the component revealed that the Brazilian manager had in fact worked with the rigid German management structure, but in a typically flexible Brazilian way. He had used the German process as a guide rather than a set procedure, only ordering the component at a late stage because he was aware of production difficulties at the manufacturing plant where it was produced, and early ordering would not have solved the problem. As he knew from personal contact that one of the German parent company's suppliers had an over-capacity that was not apparent on the online system, he had relied on the social network. He had considered both the social and the organizational processes as a means to achieve a solution to the problem. This was seen as a breach of procedure by the German parent company. The Brazilians, however, saw the rigor of German planning as inflexible. Here again, the three strands (social, organizational and technical) worked at cross-purposes.

In the German company, however, these procurement processes run smoothly because the strands are mutually reinforcing. There is no misalignment and therefore no potential for conflicts of interest.

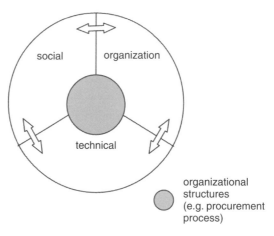

FIGURE 4.3 *German parent company: Coupled systems as shapers of organizational outcomes*

Processes in Brazilian companies also reflect the interaction of these three coupled systems. In this case, trust in and reliance on social networks may dictate a preference for solutions that are not aligned with the more procedurally rigid organizational solutions embedded in the architecture of the organization.

# CROSS-CULTURAL POTENTIAL FOR CONFLICT: LOYALTY AND IMPUNITY

## CASE 10: MAKING INVISIBLE DYNAMICS VISIBLE

### CHANGE OF PRODUCTION SCHEDULE

Brazil belongs to so-called collectivist cultures where the well-being of the group as a whole is valued much more highly than individual satisfaction. Harmony in such groups is extremely important; open confrontation is seen as loss of face and social capital. Cultural studies further contend that in collectivist societies, power is distributed very unequally and very hierarchical power structures in companies are particularly evident. The social and psychological distance between employees and superiors tends to be greater and employees are not involved in decision-making. However, they are extremely loyal to their bosses and there is an expectation that this will be reciprocated. (The concept of loyalty has its origin in the colonial system.) Formal behaviour and recognition of status are important shapers of behaviour. Conflicts of loyalty arise that affect how mistakes are dealt with. In such a context, the boss cannot be seen to single out a subordinate for blame without being seen to renege on an unwritten contract of loyalty: it is simply not done without jeopardizing the whole basis of cohesion within the extended group within the organization.

This is an area of relevance to many system managers in different industries, since knowledge of, and adequate response to, errors is an issue of concern because of:

- an impact on cost and competitiveness;
- the apparent inability of some plants to acknowledge individual error, or act decisively and at the right time as expected;
- a history of such problems that suggested to European managers either incompetence or lack of concern for the efficiency of the system;
- worsening relations between central and local management as a result of repeated exchanges on this matter.

### The problem

As in the previous example, the introduction of a special car model to the Brazilian market caused a shortage of some parts. According to the production schedule, the planning manager checked the inventory and the requirements for new parts. The quantity of parts to be ordered was twice as much as the stipulated allocation. He requested an increase in this, which was rejected due to a bottleneck in the supplier's production in Germany. In the subsequent course of events, he checked whether a similar part was in stock. It was. He checked if this part was compatible and could be used in production. It could, so he then adapted the production schedule and sent the decision to use this part to the central logistics team in Latin America.

During the start of the production run, an error occurred. The quantity of the part in question in the warehouse did not correspond to the amount required, although this had previously been checked through the inventory. This was a serious scenario, which could have resulted in a delay on the production line or even a break in production itself. Therefore alternative procurement options were again considered.

This time flying in the parts was the only viable option and was seen as less costly than a break in production. The planning manager in charge was not held responsible for his negligence (having seriously and unnecessarily increased costs). The whole department defended him and rejected the blame given to the planning department. Responsibility was shifted to a higher level.

## The need to align people, processes and technology

This case gives a deeper insight into the invisible architecture shaping social and organizational behaviour. Although the cause of the mistake had been obvious to the head of logistics he had not confronted the planning manager with his negligence or held him formally responsible for his mistake. This would have meant loss of face to the planning manager and, at the same time, would have made employees question the behaviour of a superior expected to offer protection to a team in exchange for loyalty.

As a loyal and hardworking team member, the planning manager was afforded the impunity normally given only to senior figures whose authority and competence cannot be openly challenged. This had the following results:

- From a Brazilian perspective, the social contract that ensured the continued effective working of the team, with all its attendant advantages, had been duly secured.

- From the perspective of system performance, the error of the individual was addressed by training in procurement procedures, but for the whole team rather than the individual.

- From the perspective of the German manager, there was puzzlement and concern that no individual had been identified and held to account, raising concerns about the competence and seriousness with which the Brazilian management team was addressing the problem.

Obviously, the underlying cultural belief is that the group themselves will balance deficits without pointing out individual weakness or incompetence.

Impunity is embedded in a feedback cycle that shapes social organizational behaviour as shown in Figure 4.4.

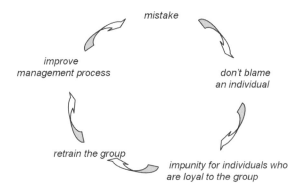

FIGURE **4.4** *Invisible architecture: The cycle of behaviour-shaping in a Brazilian organization*

**This can be seen as a recurrent scenario because it is rooted in cultural differences in the way mistakes are addressed in collective and individualist cultures. Conflict is inevitable with individualist cultures such as Germany, where little loyalty is shown to subordinates.**

## IMPLICATIONS FOR ALIGNMENT OF PEOPLE, PROCESSES AND TECHNOLOGY IN EXTENDED ENTERPRISE SYSTEMS

The cases above have looked, in particular, at two different kinds of behaviour-shaping mechanisms with the potential to impact on the cost or effectiveness of extended enterprise systems.

Our concepts of time and space, for example, frame our understanding of events in context, and therefore our choice of actions, by providing a particular filter. The way our social and cultural systems structure and validate interrelated concepts of power, social distance, loyalty and impunity shape our behaviour, and our interpretation of others' behaviour, in significantly different ways.

What are the implications of this for the designer or the manager of an extended enterprise system? In key areas of performance, it is worth being aware that these differences exist. For example, there will be differences (sometimes predictable) in:

- the interpretation of a problem;

- the perception of the most appropriate solution;

- the assumptions about how business and society work most effectively;

- the local viability of apparently standard concepts.

Cross-cultural awareness can help anticipate likely problem scenarios in particular cultures, or suggest likely explanations for variations in performance in certain areas. Cross-cultural strategies cannot solve all the problems but can help bridge the divide between these diverse communities. One approach is to provide shared spaces and opportunities.

This has been achieved in part through inter-regional training programmes, for example, where people are exchanged on placements, and multiple opportunities for cross-cultural and cross-organizational dialogue and mediation are created giving people training to raise cross-cultural awareness and developing skills (cross-cultural teamwork, cross-cultural negotiating, language training etc). Other opportunities can be created by integration of managers of target cultures into the core management group (catalytic effect) and by recruitment of people with cross-cultural experience (who can introduce a multicultural perspective).

As in the earlier case study of an extranet system design, much of the benefit comes from the social opportunities to generate shared benchmarks, terms and frames of reference within a social context, as a basis for bridging the gap between increasingly diverse and distributed communities of practice. In this context, onsite and web-based learning provided a means of increasing understanding and professional development to build on the diversity of regional expertise towards collective ends.

## FURTHER READING

Adler, Nancy J. (1991) *International Dimensions of Organizational Behavior.* Wadsworth Publishing Company, Belmont, CA.

Barbosa, Lìvia (1995) The Brazilian jeitinho: An exercise in national identity. In Hess, D. J. and DaMatta, R. A. (eds) *The Brazilian Puzzle.* Columbia University Press, New York.

Bartlett, Christopher A. and Ghoshal, Sumantra (1992) *Managing across Borders: The Transnational Solution.* Century Business, London (1st edition, 1989).

Castells, M., (1985) *The Rise of the Network Society.* Blackwell, Oxford.

De Barros, Betânia Tanure and Spyer Prates, Marco Aurélio (1996) *O Estilo Brasileiro de Administrar.* Editora Atlas, São Paulo.

Hofstede, Geert (1991) *Cultures and Organizations. Software of the Mind.* McGraw-Hill Book Company, Maidenhead.

Jaegersberg, G. (2003a) Cooperation Deutschland – Brazil in automobile and automotive supply industry. *Wirtschaftsjournal – Special 2003 – No speed limits,* pp 42–43.

Jaegersberg, G. and Ure, J. (2003) Inter-Regional Cluster Strategies: Enhancing the Competitiveness of the German Brazilian Automotive Supply Chain. Proceedings of 2nd Virtual Conference Cranfield University School of Management, Cranfield, 17–28 November. www.sck2003.com.

# 5 Strategies for Creating Value in Socio-technical Systems

When Amazon started using user profiles to actively recommend books to users, they were shaping the technology around a social process, using the web-based interface as a means of leveraging the knowledge of their user community, and seeking to convert that into competitive value. How effective this is in the case of Amazon is not yet clear; however, it is one of the most familiar examples of the approach.

The cases we have outlined so far suggest a range of strategies that align people, processes and technologies to advantage at the interfaces between the technical and the human architecture. These strategies include:

- using a common platform – designing technology around the architecture of the cognitive or social processes;

- bridging the gap – human, technical or socio-technical middleware at the interfaces where costs or value can be generated;

- creating new linkages between technical and/or human networks;

- aligning systems to create value.

Extended enterprise systems directly interface the technical and the human architecture in ways that can create costs and risks or value, and in ways that follow identifiable principles. The training traditionally provided for designers and managers of distributed web-based business systems might benefit from knowledge of recurrent socio-technical problems: solution scenarios as a means of avoiding risk or adding value. The strategic planning process for managers could also be better supported by adapting the existing toolbox to highlight local knowledge of non-technical problems.

## USING A COMMON PLATFORM

The most pervasive and probably the most generically applicable of the strategies listed above is the first one – designing technology around the architecture of the cognitive or social processes. These processes constitute a common platform at a human level, which minimizes the risk of misalignment and maximizes the potential for creating useful new linkages, or tapping the knowledge and resources of other systems. The WebSOM in Chapter 2 is an example of this in aligning cognitive and technical systems in ways which enhance sense-making in digital contexts.

# BRIDGING THE GAP

Designing or managing extended enterprise systems requires consideration of interaction and interoperability at interfaces where cost or value can be created:

- horizontally across communities in technical, social and organizational strands;
- between layers of complexity or levels of operation.

Technical interoperability often involves middleware to mediate different systems, or new and old legacy systems. This is equally applicable to social and organizational systems – where people themselves can act as intermediaries in creating shared frameworks for understanding across professional communities or national cultures.

From the perspective of system managers, professional development training that involves placements in different sites creates social and organizational infrastructure as well as technical expertise. As we have seen in the earlier cases also, it highlights the value of co-locating teams for projects requiring the sharing of expertise towards a common goal, and the reuse of established teams who have had the opportunity to bridge the gaps at the conceptual and the social level as well as the organizational and the technical level.

The computer chip is itself a series of mediating interfaces that allows information at a software level to be communicated in readable ways in the physical world. Reliable interoperability is about mediating communication in one system and communication in another, to create a new and enriched information and action space between coupled systems.

The advent of the web and human imagination has created potential socio-technical couplings and spaces that did not exist before, with an ability to generate and shape social, business, cultural and political transactions in ways that are only beginning to become apparent.

## People as middleware

Social systems have a range of mediating strategies, structures and processes for assimilating new knowledge, and developing shared constructs of action in it. Educational theories such as constructivism are rooted in this, as is the concept of web-based collaboration across communities of practice (CoPs). People provide the middleware across communities, and, in practice, professional development training with placements in different sites are often used deliberately as a strategy to enhance understanding, trust and loyalty that can act to shape future interactions in preferred ways.

Structuration theory also looks at how societies create and enact their own invisible rules of play, which they then enact and reinforce. Enactment theory in particular has drawn on these to analyse how socio-technical communities structure themselves in the absence of external controls. Chapter 6 goes into more detail (suggested further reading is listed at the end of the chapter) and highlights influential learning theories that analyse how this shaping happens at the level of the individual and at the level of the distributed system.

### Shared spaces

Families, schools, theatres all offer shared spaces in which we review, communicate, adapt or validate the soft architecture of society. Our understanding of actions in response to new information is mediated through these. Society could be described as an adaptive system acting in and on the environment with which it is coupled. Socio-technical systems such as the supply chain extend beyond the range and scale of operations for which it was originally designed.

In earlier cases, co-location of workers on cross-company projects was identified as a strategy for building better shared understanding; the exchanges mediated by people in casual social conversation in the coffee room are not built into distributed or virtual communities. Increasingly companies operating across regions incorporate professional development training that involves short-term placements in different regions as another means of mediating this gap through people.

### Shared languages

Language between different communities draws on shared metaphors as existing stepping-stones where there is no shared experience, shared terms or frames of reference. As such it is a tool for brokering value between communities who choose to collaborate towards common ends.

We saw this strategy earlier in case studies of social and business networks, where people or systems create value across what have been called structural holes in social networks by facilitating the sharing or the replication of hitherto unavailable knowledge and more informed action. Soft systems methodology, case maps and pattern languages are all established methods for mapping relationships between human and machine agents for system designers. These are often in a schematic visual form – a kind of inter-language, or middleware – bridging the language and conceptual landscapes of the technical designer and the business users.

## CREATING NEW LINKAGES BETWEEN TECHNICAL AND HUMAN NETWORKS

In social network theory, bridging these gaps or structural holes in the human architecture has been used for the optimization of communication networks in business contexts, as seen earlier. The concept of innovation clusters also draws in part on the opportunities for this kind of cross-fertilization. The advent of the web has created potential technical and socio-technical couplings, and potential socio-technical spaces that did not exist before, but whose ability to generate and shape social and business, cultural and political transactions is only beginning to become apparent.

# ALIGNING SYSTEMS TO CREATE VALUE

A range of strategies have been identified, such that existing knowledge, structures or dynamic processes can be harnessed to the advantage of the system as a whole, where possible, and to avoid gaps or ambiguities where systems interact. An additional strategy here is to raise awareness of the surprising number of recurring problem scenarios that are now recognized in the design or management of these large distributed systems.

### Obstacles to value creation

The key obstacle is the lack of awareness of recurring scenarios that cut across sectors and systems. Managers we interviewed generally expressed surprise and often relief to see that other companies had suffered the same difficulties in designing, rolling out or managing ebusiness systems. Clearly, many companies preferred not to publicize high-profile failures, costly re-design and associated additional costs.

Clearly also, the fragmented distribution of responsibilities for discrete parts of system design across stakeholding communities allows for grey areas in between, for which there is either no responsibility, or a shared one with no clear responsibilities or scoping. Identifying the missing bits is crucial here. In a volatile market, operating across unfamiliar territory, dealing with the unexpected and the unknown becomes crucial, yet is often the responsibility of no one.[1]

One of the most successful knowledge management companies in the North Sea oil industry bases its training on helping cross-sectoral project teams to identify what it is they don't know, as a first step in reengineering collaborative processes.

A second obstacle is the perception of human factors, (particularly social or cultural factors) as somehow vague, complex and hard to get a handle on. The pleasant surprise in the course of the research has been the extent to which a handful of strategies and scenarios account for a great deal of the variance, regardless of sector. It is not necessary to understand all the theoretical and practical complexities. It is necessary to know the consistent patterns that emerge from that complexity, and the specific ones that are known to arise in particular socio-technical or cross-cultural contexts. I may not understand the circuitry in my computer, or the engine in my car, but a few basic strategies allow me to bypass a fair number of the problems that may come up.

A third obstacle is the lack of a basic toolbox to put this into practice in the real world context where tangible evidence is needed. There is a pervasive view that human factors, and particularly social and cultural factors cannot be represented in tangible ways that lend themselves to consideration in the same way as, for example, financial information. Yet there are ways of ranking their impact in terms of time spent on them, or losses accrued which can be attributed to them, sufficiently to raise the profile of key issues early, and associate them with particular sites and scenarios. This is discussed further in Chapter 7.

## NOTES

1.  The American Indian story 'Who Speaks for Wolf' tells of a decision to move to a new site, which was hastily agreed by the tribal elders without consultation with the Wolf tribe. When they found themselves located in an area where wolves were a real danger to the safety of the children, they elected always to ensure everyone was fully represented in future decisions, thus limiting the danger of operating on limited information.

## FURTHER READING

Burt, R. S. (2001) Structural holes versus network closure as social capital. In Lin, N., Cook, K. and Burt, R. S. (eds) *Social Capital. Theory and Research.* Walter, New York.

Checkland, P. and Scholes, J. (1990) *Soft Systems Methodology in Action.* Wiley, Chichester.

Mumford, E. (2003) *Redesgning Human Systems.* IRM Press, Hersey, PA.

Orlikowski, W. (2002) 'Managing and Designing: Learning about Enactment', Workshop paper, MIT, May 2002. design.case.edu/2002workshop/Positions/orlikowski.doc.

Prusak, L. (1997) *Knowledge in Organisations.* Butterworth Heinemann, Boston.

# 6 The Architecture of Human Information Processing Systems

*Obtaining more powerful machines will not be the biggest problem in the future — these will come anyway — rather the issue will be to get insightful and realistic results out of them.*

*Francisco Gallo*

Aligning technical and social architectures to advantage requires some knowledge of the regularities and the dynamics of both. Training for technical managers and software system designers gives little real insight into information processing in human and biological systems.

Some approaches to system design now do draw on ethnographic methodologies from the social sciences such as collaborative action research and grounded theory. Soft systems methodology (SSM), unified modeling language (UML) use case maps and scenario planning, for example, are commonplace in requirements analysis.

Despite this, however, there is little sense of the architecture and regularities of mind and society as distributed knowledge-based systems in their own right.

## INFORMATION PROCESSING IN NATURAL SYSTEMS

In the context of the networked enterprise, distributed human and machine networks must make sense of shared information, and this knowledge is an essential precursor to effective action, and the creation of value.

Exploiting even more distributed and heterogeneous networks in future, such as grid-based web services, will require an understanding of how information is perceived, understood and converted into the kind of situated knowledge on which performance and value depends. While wishing to avoid theoretical discussions in a book of this nature, we feel that a better awareness of how our own cognitive and our social systems operate to generate, reuse and re-purpose distributed information and knowledge is central to designing or managing the technical systems that now mediate or extend these capacities. A particular problem in this respect has been the differentiation of information and knowledge, and the relationship between knowledge, action and perceived benefit. A very brief context is given here of the architecture of (a) the cognitive and (b) the social architecture that acts as a shared 'platform' for human information systems. We believe that cost-effective systems build on, and leverage, these underlying dynamics and thus require knowledge of how they operate. The very schematic overview in these pages is intended to provide a context for this, and some suggested further reading is listed at the end of the chapter.

## THE COGNITIVE PROCESS

Figure 6.1 highlights the different stages in the cognitive process as a basis for seeing where support, enhancement, alignment or intervention is possible in the stages between the perception of information and the actioning of knowledge in context.

For the purposes of this discussion, we take knowledge to be an adaptive interface between information and action. It is information applied to achieve a goal, solve a problem or enact a decision.

From the perspective of creating alignments between the architecture of technical and human systems, the model is a means of making visible:

- the **structural** architecture (e.g. the nature of cognitive information);
- the **process** architecture (e.g. from selective perception of information to knowledge generation and decision-making and situated action).

The diagram provides a simplified overview of the relationship between information, knowledge and action. For the sake of simplicity we have not included the motor aspects of perception as information is selectively attended, nor the many ways in which the cognitive and the social architecture impact on each other – the multiple feedback loops through which perception, cognition and behaviour are modulated in response to action. The intention here is to highlight the relationship between information, knowledge and action as a process, and therefore to the ways in which the process can be supported, or hindered, at different stages.

While Figure 6.1 is a vast over-simplification of a dynamic process, it serves to highlight:

- the role of concepts in structuring knowledge of relations between classes (situated understanding);
- the under-estimated role of constructs in structuring knowledge of relations between actions and outcomes, leading to situated action;
- the role of feedback from the environment in reshaping or reinforcing these in dynamic and adaptive ways;
- where and how technical, social, cultural or physical systems can interface with this process – either positively or negatively.

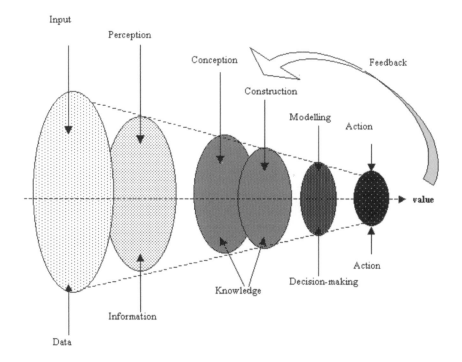

**FIGURE 6.1** *Knowledge as an adaptive interface between emerging information and action*

## Phase 1: Perception

An initial understanding of the architecture mediating perception comes from the basic building blocks of perception and cognition. Our information-processing systems do not map one-to-one with reality, but all display a deep structure, based on selection and interpretation that builds on existing knowledge and expectations. This derives from the need to process relevant information as rapidly as possible as the basis for action – much as the reuse of patterns and frameworks in software design can cut cost, time and risk.

For human information systems, speed of response and accuracy of response evolved iteratively as a means of survival in a hostile environment. They continue to evolve in tandem with networked technology, in the equally competitive forces of the competitive global business environment.

Living organisms typically perceive and use a restricted number of underlying dimensions (tacit and explicit) to select and interpret complex information rapidly, affording competitive advantage where the speed and accuracy with which knowledge can be created, transferred and acted on is crucial. The following sections suggest how this happens, and why sampling reality makes it difficult to transfer knowledge across wider communities where there is no explicitly shared framework, and how crucial changes in the external environment are assimilated and accommodated in cellular or social networks.

The basic unit of perception is similarity and difference, around which we build dimensions of difference that are the building blocks for understanding and action. The building block for cognition is the concept or schema. The building block for action or behaviour is the construct.

Given that information systems have limited capacity for processing information, the abstracting of information into a manageable number of dimensions is a feature of all theories of human information processing. The architecture of individual knowing, both explicit and tacit, starts with the building blocks and the relationships between them.

## Phase 2: Conceptual architecture

Conceptual maps of semantically similar clusters solve a lot of problems for human information processing systems with limited capacity, limited information, or limited time. They allow users to operate rapidly and cost-effectively by performing operations on a manageable set of higher order concepts, zooming into the level of detail only when necessary. (Visual perception also operates this way, scanning and zooming in on target areas rather than processing the entire field.) This allows for constant accommodation and assimilation as new information is processed and validated against existing examples in each conceptual category. The existence of other examples can provide a benchmark for evaluating the likely validity of new information or the need to extend or adapt the defining characteristic of a particular category.

The existence of other users provides a further avenue for validating, acquiring or interpreting new or unexpected information.

## Interoperability in human information systems

The recurrence of particular solutions to the problem of knowledge representation and knowledge-sharing across natural systems may have implications for the design of knowledge management systems in socio-technical contexts such as intranets, portals, supply chains and so on.

In natural information and communication systems there are generic features that mirror those created in software systems:

- elements (e.g. actors, objects and concepts);
- constructed relationships;
- multiple perspectives.

A core of underlying categories for parsing our experience of the world appears to be part of a generic architecture, which lends itself to reuse by technical system designers. Action workflow maps, for example, have agents and relationships which are analogous to these.

## Phase 3: Constructing and modelling action

Societies, communities and cultures invest a great deal of capital, social and other, in maintaining, and occasionally adapting, shared bases. A great deal of variation in performance is not accounted for by differences in basic knowledge, but in our constructions of how to act on that knowledge to achieve particular ends. The different constructions of Brazilian and German operators in the automotive manufacturing supply chain in Chapter 4 are a case in point.

In business systems, speed, cost and added value of new knowledge is paramount. However, receiving information is several steps away from making sense of it and implementing that knowledge in practice in ways that create value. Currently, networked systems succeed in extending the information available, but there is a need for more consideration of how users will convert that into actionable knowledge towards shared ends.

## Knowledge is not the problem

In interviewing technology managers and business managers, it became clear that a perfect knowledge of each others' areas of expertise would, in itself, have done little to alter the choice of design solutions for extended enterprise systems. Both groups typically had different aims, different criteria for success and different bases for reward and reinforcement. It was these which ultimately dictated preferred design and management solutions. The promotion of preferred options, associated with particular benefits for the contenders, was often a socio-political process. Knowledge here was more for support than illumination unless very strict criteria had been drawn up in advance, and strictly adhered to.

## From concept maps to construct maps

While everyone is familiar with the concept map as means of sharing conceptual knowledge, fewer people are aware that similar mappings (construct maps) can be used to map our constructions of relationships between actions and outcomes and to generate mental models. These models of how things work strongly influence the way we act on knowledge, yet they are often unconscious. They are also strongly shaped by both experience (first- and second-hand) and by the models held by our personal, professional or cultural communities – this is where cross-cultural differences impact most.

By explicitly defining constructs of how we think things work, we become aware of multiple views. These are often implicit, and rooted in very different personal, professional and cultural experiences and beliefs. The professional cultures of marketing managers and those of software designers, for example, are built on very different models of effective action, and very different criteria of what constitutes a successful outcome.

Even if the two groups were to agree on the best course of action, the actual outcomes would also be judged on very different criteria.

## Social and socio-technical architecture

> Social capital makes possible the achievement of ends that would be impossible without it, or that could be achieved only at extra cost.
>
> NAHAPIET and GHOSHAL, '*Social capital, intellectual capital and the organizational advantage*', 2000

As suggested earlier, social systems are also distributed, agent-based information systems, designed iteratively over time to be cost-effective in the generation, sharing and reuse of knowledge in a competitive and volatile environment.

Human concepts such as trust can be construed as strategic responses to these challenges (e.g. trust has been interpreted as a means of optimizing outcomes and minimizing risk on the basis of past experience). As networked systems increasingly replace or extend the range and nature of social transactions they can benefit from building on this existing architecture.

Designing or aligning distributed technical and human networks to advantage requires some knowledge of the regularities and the dynamics of both. Existing knowledge of how this can be managed is fragmented across theoretical disciplines.

Actor network theory, social network theory, structuration theory, enactment theory and dynamic systems theory are among a range of theoretical approaches to the social architecture as a system, and a grammar with useful principles and regularities.

Increasingly, the solutions from distributed systems in nature are providing models for what have come to be called distributed agent-based networks, where agents may be human or technical, and where the system as a whole must adapt itself to volatile and competitive environments. It is perhaps not surprising that survival in volatile physical and social environments has shaped the visible and the invisible architecture of biological systems in ways that have implications for socio-technical systems.

Technical and semantic 'interoperability' are already well-established as concepts. The interoperability of human and technical networks is still a fragmented field, however, despite the huge costs and risks associated with technically sound designs that fail to survive their first encounter with their human operating systems.

# IMPLICATIONS FOR DESIGN AND MANAGEMENT OF SOCIO-TECHNICAL SYSTEMS

Some of the examples in this book adopt the strategy of building the technology around knowledge of the cognitive software we already have. For instance, we categorize and represent what we know in terms of similarities and differences. Concept maps organize information in this way. Similar concepts are located in cognate sets, and make information retrieval faster and more cost-effective by a range of reinforcing mechanisms that draw on our own conceptual software.

Extended enterprise networks go beyond the reach of the evolutionary mechanisms by which social groupings facilitate, modify and reinforce their shared bases. (Socialization, acculturation, development of shared values, the reinforcement of particular behaviour, the rooting of this in shared stories, scenarios and roles.) The works of Piaget and Vygotsky are primary sources for this, as are the works of recent authors drawing on the structuration of behaviour in distributed social networks from insect colonies to terrorist networks and military agents in the field. Some of these are listed in the Further Reading section. While many are highly specialized and technical, they represent some of the most fascinating cross-disciplinary sources for socio-technical systems design and management. They are made compelling by the fact that they describe iterative natural solutions to the difficulties inherent in designing or managing distributed agent-based systems in a competitive and volatile environment.

Networked systems have to compensate for the lack of a social glue to create shared contexts, shared frames of reference. A shared stage with known roles and preferred outcomes needs to be either hard-wired genetically, or explicitly fostered by social, organizational or technical means if distributed actions and distributed knowledge are to be harnessed to advantage.

The cases clearly showed, for example, that by explicitly defining or co-creating generic frames of reference, collaborating project teams are more likely to be able to make collective sense of distributed knowledge across different departmental and professional cultures.

At one end of the design spectrum this may take the form of constraining actions to fit pre-defined technical parameters where there is little scope for human input – neither adding nor subtracting value. In others it may take the form of identifying useful cognitive, social or cultural dynamics and using technology to extend or enhance these – adding value by harnessing existing forces, but with an element of risk. This corresponds to Hutchens's approach of cognitive enhancement, or Burt's approach to social network theory – mapping information in terms of meaningful social structures to support sense-making and contingent action in context.

In terms of management, shaping or enhancing organizational behaviour around preferred outcomes is not only about mapping and aligning knowledge; it is also about mapping and aligning appropriate action. This can be mapped equally well, and is in other disciplines. Moreover, it provides a missing link with the socio-political dynamics that is patently a factor in decision-making.

## Mapping knowledge and constructed actions

Concept maps have been one of the most pervasively used web-based systems for supporting collective knowledge-sharing in this way: their intuitive effectiveness builds on the cognitive architecture of information processing. Their migration from paper to web has allowed them to aid collective knowledge-sharing and knowledge-building across distributed networks in ways not previously possible. This has created a genuinely socio-technical tool that uses the storage and communication capacity of networked systems, and the rich diversity of distributed knowledge across multiple professional communities within a defined conceptual frame of reference.

Construct maps have similar potential for making the invisible visible, and supporting discussion of the benefits of particular choices of action for particular stakeholding groups. While some of this is exploited in decision-making tools such as Banxia (www.banxia.com), this is surprisingly under-utilized in business, as compared with other disciplines.

Just as concept maps highlight differences in perceived relationships, construct maps can highlight differences in perceived relationships between actions, outcomes and benefits. In other practice based contexts such as education, psychology and nursing, this is a long-established basis for enhancing individual or organizational performance through discussion with peers or expert others.

Networked organizations are increasingly seen as having the potential to create value through social capital, yet the mechanisms whereby this can be achieved are not clearly articulated in ways that are specific enough for system designers or managers. Where examples exist, the principal strategy is to build on the existing architecture of human systems. A prominent example here is Burt's mapping of social communication networks within or between organizations, as a basis of identifying structural holes, the bridging of which creates exchange and value.

However, these also have to go beyond consideration of information and knowledge, and include consideration of the different constructions of appropriate action, and the socio-political constraints and dynamics of implementing it in practice.

# FURTHER READING

Bannister, D. and Fransella, F. (1986) *Inquiring Man: Psychology of Personal Constructs.* 3rd edition. Croom Helm, London.

Bourdieu, P. (1986) The forms of capital. In Richardson, J. G. (ed.) *Handbook of Theory and Research for the sociology of Education.* Greenwood, New York.

Burt, R. S. (1992) *Structural Holes: The Social Structure of Competition.* Harvard University Press, Cambridge, MA.

Davis, M., Denning, K., Watkins, K. and Milton, J. (2000) Virtual learning communities: Creating meaning through dialogue and enquiry in cyberspace. Procedings of ALT-C 2000 Conference, Edinburgh.

De Barros, Betânia Tanure e Spyer Prates, Marco Aurélio (1996), *O Estilo Brasileiro de Administrar.* São Paulo: Editora Atlas.

Hutchens, I. (1995) *Cognition in the Wild.* MIT Press, Cambridge, MA.

Jaegersberg, G., Lloyd, A. D., Dewar, R. G., Pooley, R. J. and Ure, J. (2001). Managing Socio-technical Processes in the Supply Chain. Proceedings of Supply Chain Knowledge Conference 2001, Cranfield School of Management, Cranfield.

Kelly, G. A. (1963) *A Theory of Personality: The Psychology of Personal Constructs.* W.W. Norton, New York.

Kogut, B. and Zander, U. (1996) What do firms do? Coordination, identity and learning. *Organization Science* 7: 502–518.

Latour, Bruno (1986) Visualization and cognition: Thinking with eyes and hands. *Knowledge and Society: Studies in the Sociology of Culture Past and Present* 6: 1–40.

Latour, Bruno (1996) Social theory and the study of computerized work sites. In Orlikowski, W. J., Walsham, G., Jones, M. R. and DeGross, J. I. (eds) *Information Technology and Changes in Organizational Work.* Chapman & Hall, London.

Maturana, H. and Varela, F. (1998) *The Tree of Knowledge: The Biological Roots of Human Understanding.* Shambhala, Boston.

McClelland, J. L. and Rumelhart, D. E. (eds) (1986) *Parallel Distributed Processing: Explorations in the Microstructure of Cognition. Vol. 2: Psychological and Biological Models.* MIT Press, Cambridge.

Nahapiet, J. and Ghoshal, S. (2000) Social capital, intellectual capital and the organizational advantage. In Lesser, E. L. *Knowledge and Social Capital.* Butterworth Heineman, Boston.

Novak, J. D. and Gowin, D. B. (1984) *Learning How to Learn.* Cambridge University Press, New York and Cambridge.

Orlikowski, W. (2002) 'Managing and Designing: Learning about Enactment', Workshop paper, MIT, May 2002. design.case.edu/2002workshop/Positions/orlikowski.doc.

Piaget, J. (1970) *The Science of Education and the Psychology of the Child.* Grossman, New York.

Rocha, L. M. (1998) Where is the progress? *Cybernetics and Human Knowing.* 5(4): 86–90.

Segel, L. A. and Cohen, I. R. (2001) *Design Principles for the Immune System and Other Distributed Autonomous Systems.* Santa Fe Institute Studies in the Sciences of Complexity, Oxford University Press Oxford.

Suchman, L. (1987) *Plans and Situated Actions: The Problem of Human–Machine Communication.* Cambridge University Press, New York.

Vygotsky, L. S. (1978) *Mind in Society.* Harvard University Press, Cambridge, MA.

Wenger, E. and Snyder, W. (2002) Communities of practice: The organizational frontier. *Harvard Business Review* January/February: 139–145.

Wolf, Randall P. (1998) Knowledge acquisition via the integration of personal constructs and conceptual graphs. PhD dissertation, Computer Science Department, University of Alabama, Huntsville, AL.

# 7 Implications for Designers and Managers of Socio-technical Systems

*'System archetypes' or 'generic structures' embody the key to learning to see structures in our personal and organizational lives. The systems archetypes – of which there are only a relatively small number – suggest that not all management problems are unique, something that experienced managers know intuitively ... Just as in literature there are common themes and recurring plot lines that get recast with different characters and settings, a relatively small number of these archetypes are common to a very large variety of management situations.*

*Peter Senge, The Fifth Discipline, 1990, p. 94.*

## SEEING THE INVISIBLE ARCHITECTURE

Extended enterprise systems increasingly support working relationships with external groups whose cooperation is central to competitiveness, such as first-, second- and third-tier suppliers, companies to whom aspects of the business have been outsourced, and staff in partner organizations. As technology extends the potential for collaborative partnerships, it extends the need for seeing how interrelated social, organizational and culturally defined processes can be mapped and managed in ways that create value rather than costs. 'Seeing' the cognitive and the social processes in action in familiar contexts makes it easier to identify recurring dynamics of this 'invisible architecture' and evaluate the impact of different strategies for mapping and managing it to advantage. We need to:

- make soft processes more visible by mapping concepts, constructs and networks;
- make them more tangible by ranking and weighting;
- integrate measures of soft processes into the strategic management toolbox.

In complex systems covering multiple organizational, geographical, cultural and political communities, the impact of non-technical processes on competitiveness is increasingly an issue of concern. In industry groups such as the automotive and oil and gas industry, variations in performance across sites in collaborative enterprises are a particularly crucial component in competitiveness – yet there is little in traditional training to highlight either awareness of, or strategies for, aligning distributed human and technical systems to advantage in this way.

Social networks are distributed information systems in their own right, with architecture capable of operating in volatile environments, and with incomplete information. They filter, reconfigure, reconstruct, adapt and implement distributed knowledge to collective ends in ways which offer both opportunities and challenges to system designers and managers.

We have tried to highlight a range of strategies to leverage the collective technical and human resource to business advantage, such as:

- enhancing the reach of the cognitive, the social or the cultural process for sharing or reconstructing knowledge;

- building technological systems around the cognitive or the social network;

- mapping distributed cognitive or social behaviour in networks, as a basis for enhancing or interpreting outcomes;

- identifying recurring socio-technical dynamics that can inform choices in the design or management of distributed networked systems.

## IMPLICATIONS FOR TOOLS AND TRAINING

There would seem to be an argument for the development and use of case studies in professional development as a means of putting recurrent scenarios in a real and rich context for comparison, analysis and discussion. Currently, awareness of the impact of socio-technical problems on competitiveness is not matched by coherent guidelines for identifying and dealing with them.

In addition, dependence on largely quantitative tools (e.g. indices of financial costs or technical interoperability) could provide managers in any technically mediated system with a potentially costly and misleading misrepresentation of the emerging risks and opportunities. The capture and transfer of tacit knowledge of less tangible social or socio-technical processes in the different domains in the supply chain is arguably a necessary element in the effective design and management of these closely associated systems. The 'dark continent' in the knowledge available for supporting decisions in the design and management of the supply chain is increasingly an issue of concern to senior management and there are numerous examples in practice of the potential cost of planning based on limited knowledge.

As networked systems straddle organizations and countries, they increasingly connect disparate groups who cannot safely be assumed to share common bases for understanding or for preferred actions. 'Common sense' in one context may be neither 'common' nor 'sensible' in another, where beliefs, interpretations and contexts for application are different. The tacit knowledge that could inform better design and management of processes and systems in the supply chain is in the system; however, existing supply chain improvement tools currently are geared to mapping more explicit and easily quantifiable knowledge.

Observations during supply chain improvement workshops in the UK, Germany and Brazil suggest that although a wide range of tools were evident as a means of ranking, categorizing, analysing and planning, the capture and coding of knowledge for inclusion in the planning process were used almost exclusively with quantifiable data such as costs from particular domains. However, research suggests that a major impediment to competitiveness in ICT-dependent organizations can be a lack of access to knowledge about interdependencies between technical, social, organizational and cultural systems.

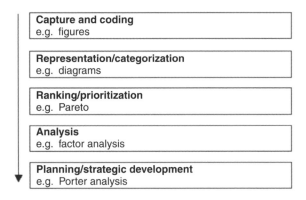

**Figure 7.1** *Typical supply chain improvement tools*

Figure 7.1 summarizes the typical elements in the strategic managers' toolbox. The list is derived from a set used in workshops to enhance supply chain management in a consortium of oil companies.

The major problem with including so-called soft processes in system design and management is the perception that these cannot be captured for use with other quantitative measures. The default strategy in practice has often been to leave them out altogether. One way round this is to use subjective rankings or weightings to generate the kind of quantitative measures that are compatible with the type of tools that are already in use. In addition to quantitative feedback normally requested from distributed centres, it should be possible to request rankings of the costs incurred and the time spent on non-technical management processes. These would go some way to providing the kind of early warning system that is lacking in many extended systems. Additionally they would give a profile of emerging areas of cost and risk which could inform design management or planning priorities.

The typical tools for ranking (e.g. Pareto), prioritization (e.g. opportunity potential assessment tools) and strategic planning (e.g. Porter analysis and Boston Matrix analysis), can be used with qualitative data as well as quantitative data (if this is captured and coded in the first instance). Extending use in this way allows a more realistic inclusion of the resources required to address the non-technical issues in the supply chain and, perhaps, a more insightful focus on the less obvious factors affecting the cost-effectiveness of the supply chain.

## CONCLUSION

Funding agencies are increasingly looking at research on the potential for synergies between social and technical systems – particularly in terms of knowledge sharing and knowledge generation in distributed systems. The thrust of research and development is moving from concerns about technical interoperability to semantic interoperability between distributed communities and synergies between coupled systems.

We hope that these cases go some way to raising awareness of the nature and impact of interaction between distributed technical and human systems – both as a challenge and an opportunity. They are intended to highlight the fact that there are tangible structures and dynamics in socio-technical systems and also recurring scenarios which have the potential to cut costs, cut risks and add value in what is an increasingly high cost, high risk endeavour. The comments of managers suggest the need for dissemination of a wider range of strategies and tools at the level of system design and strategic management, as well as a greater use of socio-technical cases studies in undergraduate training and professional development.

## FURTHER READING

Berners-Lee, T., Hendler, J. and Lassila, O. (2001) The semantic web. *Scientific American* May: 34–43.

De Roure, D., Jennings, N. R. and Shadbolt, N. R. (2001) Research agenda for the semantic grid: A future e-science infrastructure. Report for EPSRC/DTI e-Science Core Programme, National e-Science Centre University of Southampton.

Senge, P., Kleiner, A., Roberts, C., Ross, R. B. and Smith, B. J. (1994) *Fifth Discipline Fieldbook: Strategies for Building a Learning Organization*. Nicholas Brealey Publishing, London.

Woolgar, S. (2003) Social shaping perspectives on e-science and e-social science: The case for research support. A consultative study for the Economic and Social Research Council (ESRC) University of Southampton. Unpublished.

# Appendix: Glossary of Theoretical Terms

## SOCIAL NETWORK THEORY AND ANALYSIS

Social network theory is a relational approach that takes the unit of analysis to be the set of elements and relationships and their properties, as opposed to the properties of the individual elements. It analyses the structure of relationships between individuals, groups or organizations and relates this to behaviour or beliefs. The analysis techniques may refer to different aspects of the communication structures of organizations such as:

- communication patterns;
- identification of groups;
- communication roles (e.g. gatekeepers) and types.

It is associated with the original work of Barnes in 1954 on social networks in Norway, and the work of Rogers in 1986 on communication theory and the work of Burt (1992) on the ways in which value can be added through analysis of communication flows in existing social and business networks. A raft of new work is now emerging here in social psychology, communications and business. Castells' *The Rise of the Network Society* (1985) is one of the more salient publications that build on this conceptualization.

Knowledge of these structures can help predict or explain outcomes, or likely relationships between nodes, where no data is available. For example, in a business context, there may be efficient but invisible networks of informal communication that explain organizational behaviour not evident from an analysis of the more visible formal channels of communication.

If the organization can be represented as a network of actors, then structure, form and the effects of technology can be represented by describing the links (human and computer-based) between these actors. This has obvious applications in networked systems where both human and technical dynamics and relationships need to be considered.

It is fair to say that social network theory has provided a new set of tools for analysis of socio-technical systems where the role of culture, power, norms, expectations and so forth need to be included. A range of applications is overviewed in Monge and Contractor (2003).

# STRUCTURATION AND ADAPTIVE STRUCTURATION THEORY (AST)

This is derived from Anthony Giddens's structuration theory in 1984, and has increasingly been used to study the role of information systems on organizational change. The theory views groups or organizations as systems where the members create the structures that produce and reproduce it. It focuses on the ways in which the members of social systems themselves create and recreate the invisible architecture of the system which regulates and coordinates behaviour. Systems and structures are seen as acting to reinforce and recreate each other.

An outside observer might wonder, for example, why drivers follow certain rules at lights and crossings where physical architecture does not constrain options. The theory deals with the observation that members of social groups produce, reproduce and observe agreed rules that are not evident to those external to it.

This has been applied to the understanding of social systems that are mediated by technical systems, and where both are potential actors in a complex 'coupled' system geared to competitive ends. In this, the works of DeSanctis and Poole (1994) and Orlikowski (2002) have been particularly influential.

At a level below, developmental psychologists such as Vygotsky have already established theories that deal with the ways in which these rules and regulations can then be disseminated and validated within society as part of the development and the cultural process of 'assisted learning' within the family or through interaction with significant others.

At a level above, the emergence of structure in initial system states has long-term implications for subsequent development, and this provides a link with more general theories of complex systems (see Systems Theory below).

There are interesting parallels with complex adaptive systems in nature, such as ant colonies where structure also evolves through complex interaction in a distributed and autonomous system (Segel and Cohen, 2001). Distributed self-regulating in nature, systems provide continuity, coordination and are adaptive – producing new rules and structures in response to external change, without the need for external direction.

Increasingly, system designers are looking at the evolutionary strategies evident in natural systems to achieve this degree of stability and flexibility in the context of volatile and competitive markets. Increasingly, experimental work in this area is based on system simulation of large agent-based systems of human and non-human agents cooperating in a shared environment such as the internet or the grid to achieve a task.

# ENACTMENT THEORY

Enactment theory follows on from this. It is a view of social construction in which the action itself brings into existence structures and events. It suggests that systems and organizations achieve continuity and stability in the coordination of behaviour by the 'enactment' of those rules and patterns of behaviour that have already been established. As in structuration theory, the social system itself both produces and reproduces the behaviour that creates it. It is associated with Weick (1995) in the context of business organizations, and with Orlikowski (2002) in the context of the use of technology in business contexts.

An interesting parallel comes from the 'songlines' in Aboriginal society in Australia where the world has to be ritually sung into existence, or enacted, with each tribe responsible for the preservation of the part of the song relating to their own geographical area, and the Dreamtime ancestors that created it. Without this enactment, the world of the Dreamtime would disappear according to the traditional belief system, together with all the embedded geographical, social and cultural rules for travel, trade and interaction (Chatwin, 1998).

Enactment theory is consonant with other theories on the emergence of structure in other distributed networked systems (see Systems Theory below).

# ACTOR NETWORK THEORY (ANT)

Actor network theory is an influential theory (abbreviated as ANT) initiated by Bruno Latour and Michael Callon (1992) in the Ecole des Mines in Paris, France. It focuses attention on the networks that engineers and scientists create to get their projects done. These networks involve a range of different resources, agents (e.g. human or computer agents) and types of capital (e.g. social capital).

It has provided an array of concepts for describing the development, design and management of science and technology in society, and a systematic way of bringing out the invisible infrastructure of other resources that contribute to scientific and technological achievement. It relates to theories such as structuration theory and enactment theory in that it derives from an analysis of the negotiation and representation of identities, roles and strategies of interaction between agents in a social network.

The most important of these negotiations is translation, in which actors:

- construct common definitions and meanings;
- define representivities;
- co-opt each other to achieve objectives.

ANT differs from other sociological approaches in that it makes little distinction between human and non-human actors or actants. It is also unusual in that it does not assume that the beliefs and actions of actors can be pre-determined. In this there are interesting potential links to theories of dynamic systems design, and the means by which stable or recurring patterns of behaviour develop in complex, dynamic, agent-based systems in biology, defence and business systems involving networks of human and technical agents.

A range of definitions from well-known figures in the field (Jay Lemke, Michael Goguen, Michael Callon and Thierry Bardini) are available on carbon.cudenver.edu/~mryder_data/ant_dff.html.

## SYSTEMS THEORY

Sytems theory is a cross-disciplinary approach, which has come particularly to the fore in the analysis of complex and adaptive systems in nature (e.g. ant colonies, neural networks) and in society (e.g. global business systems, agent-based defence systems).

The theory argues that even in very complex systems there is organization, and there are stable patterns of behaviour, regardless of the domain. The underlying rules through which these regularities are created are seen as central to the understanding, design or management of the wide range of systems in nature and society which are complex, adaptive and self-regulating.

There are overlaps here with those theories already mentioned, which deal with the structuring and the enactment of behaviour within systems. Systems theory is, however, more concerned with the behaviour of the system as a whole in response to these and other factors.

Networked business systems are among the complex networks that can be looked at from this standpoint, in that they now encompass very complex, coupled technical and human networks that adapt to changing local and global needs. In this DeSanctis and Poole (1994) are seminal authors.

More traditional and deterministic approaches that have been useful at a local level have failed to provide a reliable means of anticipating or managing the behaviour of such systems at the global scale. This has fuelled a series of related theoretical developments (cybernetics, systems theory, dynamical systems theory and agent-based systems) on the structure and function of such systems.

Grid-based systems currently provide a central arena for this, having moved from the challenge of designing and managing the technical interoperability to the challenge of operating across different communities, with different perspectives, aims and modus operandi.

## SOCIO-TECHNICAL SYSTEMS

The socio-technical systems movement addresses the role of social and technical dynamics in determining the outcome of work-based systems. It grew originally from the early work of Mumford (2003), Pasmore (1988) and Trist (1981) in the English coal mining industry, where mechanization had decreased productivity. Trist proposed that manufacturing and other systems involve the interconnection of both human and technical strands to determine performance. The work of this group at the Tavistock Institute has since been applied to networked information and communications technologies in business and other systems.

Extended networked systems in business contexts depend heavily on the coordination of both technical and human systems across multiple organizations. While the technical interoperability of these systems has been addressed to a large extent, the interoperability of human networks (cognitive, social, semantic, cultural) has only come to the fore as the cost of ignoring it has become apparent.

As with other complex adaptive and distributed systems, socio-technical systems display regularities that can be of use to system designers and managers seeking to build on known synergies and avoid known risks in what is a high cost, high risk enterprise. This book uses case studies to highlight the impact of failing to address business systems as coupled systems, and the potential for aligning them to competitive advantage. Taylor and Felten (1992) also look at this in an American context.

# Further Reading

Ackerman, M., Volmar, P. and Volker, W. (2003) *Sharing Expertise: Beyond Knowledge Management*. MIT Press, Cambridge, MA.

Adler, N. J. (1991) *International Dimensions of Organizational Behavior*. Wadsworth Publishing Company, Belmont/California.

Bannister, D. and Fransella, F. (1986) *Inquiring Man: Psychology of Personal Constructs*. 3rd edition. Croom Helm, London.

Barbosa, L. (1992) *O Jeitinho Brasileiro. A Arte de ser mais Igual que os Outros*. 6th Edition. Editora Campus, Rio de Janeiro.

Barbosa, L. (1995) The Brazilian Jeitinho: An exercise in national identity. In Hess, D. J. and DaMatta, R. A. (eds) *The Brazilian Puzzle*. Columbia University Press, New York.

Barnes, J. (1954) Class and committees in a Norwegian island parish, *Human Relations*, 39–58.

Bartlett, C. A. and Ghoshal, S. (1992) *Managing Across Borders. The Transnational Solution*. Century Business, London (1st edition, 1989).

Bates, T. (1999) Managing Technological Change: Strategies for University and College Leaders, Jossey Bass, San Francisco. bates.cstudies.ubc.ca/bates.htm.

Berger, P. L. and Luckmann, T. (1966) *The Social Construction of Reality: A Treatise in the Social Construction of Reality*. Doubleday, New York.

Berners-Lee, T., Hendler, J. and Lassila, O. (2001) The semantic web. *Scientific American*. May, pp 34–43.

Bijker, W. E., Hughes, T. P. and Pinch, T. F. (1989) The social construction of technological systems: New Directions. In Bijker, W. and Law, J. (eds) *Shaping Technology, Building Society: Studies in Sociotechnical Change*. MIT Press, Cambridge, Mass.

Boisot, M. (1998) *Knowledge Assets: Securing Competitive Advantage in the Information Economy*. Oxford University Press, Oxford.

Bourdieu, P. (1986) The forms of human capital. In Richardson, J. G. (ed) *Handbook of Theory and Research For the Sociology of Education*. Greenwood, New York.

British Computer Society Sociotechnical Group Archive www.sociotechnical.org/London_prev_lect.htm. in *Sociology and History of Technology*, MIT Press, Cambridge.

Budd, J., Vanka, S. and Runton, A. (1999) The ID-online asynchronous learning network: A 'Virtual Studio' for interdisciplinary design collaboration. *Digital Creativity*, 10 (4), 205–214.

Burt, R. S. (1992) *Structural Holes: The Social Structure of Competition*. Harvard University Press, Cambridge, MA.

Burt, R. S. (2001) Structural holes versus network closure as social capital. In Lin, N., Cook, K., and Burt, R. S., (eds) *Social Capital. Theory and Research*. Walter, New York.

Bush, V. (1945) As we may think. *Atlantic Monthly*, 176, 101–108.

Callon, M. and Latour, B. (1992) Don't throw the baby out with the Bath School! A Reply to Collins and Yearley. In Pickering, A. (ed.) *Science as Practice and Culture*. University of Chicago Press, Chicago.

Cañas, A. J. and Carvalho, M. (2004) Concept Maps and AI: an Unlikely Marriage? Proceedings of SBIE 2004: Simpósio Brasileiro de Informática na Educação, Manaus, Brazil, 09–12 November. www.ihmc.us/users/acanas/Publications/ConceptMapsAI/Canas-CmapsAI-Sbie2004.pdf.

Castells, M. (1985) *The Rise of the Network Society*. Blackwells, Oxford.

Chatwin, B. (1998) *The Songlines*. Vintage, London.

Checkland, P. and Scholes, J. (1990) *Soft Systems Methodology in Action*. Wiley, Chichester.

Christopher, M. (1998) *Logistics and Supply Chain Management: Strategies for Reducing Cost and Improving Service*. Prentice Hall, London.

Coakes, E., Willis, D. and Clarke, S. (eds) (2001) *Knowledge Management in the Sociotechnical World: The Graffiti Continues*. Springer Verlag, London.

Comfort, L. (2000) Anticipating fire: A sociotechnical approach to mitigation, *Technology*, **7**, 33–42.

Coplien, J. (1997) Organizational Patterns. www.bell-labs.com/cgi-user/OrgPatterns/OrgPatterns.

DaMatta, R. (1997) *Carnavais, Manlandros e Heróis*. 6th edition. Rocco, Rio de Janeiro.

DaMatta, R. (1998) *O que Faz o Brasil, Brasil?* Rocco, Rio de Janeiro.

Davenport, T. H. and Probst, J. B. (2002) *Knowledge Management Case Book: Siemens Best Practices*. Wiley, Chichester.

Davis, M., Denning, K., Watkins, K. and Milton, J. (2000) Virtual Learning Communities: creating meaning through dialogue and enquiry in cyberspace. Proceedings of ALT-C 2000 Conference, Manchester, 11–13 September.

De Barros, B. T. and Spyer Prates, M. A. (1996) *O Estilo Brasileiro de Administrar*. Editora Atlas, São Paulo.

De Roure, D., Jennings, N. R. and Shadbolt, N. R. (2001*) Research Agenda for the Semantic Grid: A Future e-Science Infrastructure*. Technical Report, National e-Science Centre, Report for EPSRC/DTI e-Science Core Programme University of Southampton.

DeSanctis, G. and Poole, M. S. (1994) Capturing the complexity in advanced technology use: Adaptive structuration theory. *Organisation Science*, 5, 121–147.

Dewar, R., Lloyd, A. D., Pooley, R. and Stevens, P. (1999) Identifying and communicating expertise in systems reengineering: A patterns approach. *IEE Proceedings-Software*, 146 (3), 145–152.

Dillon, A. (2000) Group dynamics meets cognition: Combining socio-technical concepts and usability engineering in the design of information systems. In Coakes, E. et al. (eds) *The New Sociotech: Graffitti On the Long Wall*, CSCW Series, Springer Verlag, London.

Dyer, J. H. (2000) *Collaborative Advantage. Winning Through Extended Enterprise Supplier Networks*. Oxford University Press, Oxford.

Foster, I. and Kesselman, C. (eds) (2004) *The Grid: Blueprint for a New Computing Infrastructure*. Morgan-Kaufmann, London.

Foucault, M. (1980) *Power/Knowledge – Selected Interviews and Other Writings 1972–1977*. Harvester Press, Brighton.

Galegher, J., Kraut, R. E. and Egido, C. (eds) (1991) *Intellectual Teamwork: Social and Technological Foundations of Cooperative Work*. Hillsdale N. J. Lawrence Erblaum Associates, Mahwah.

Gamma, E., Helm, R. and Johnson, R. and Vlissides, J. (1995) *Design Patterns: Elements of Reusable Object-Oriented Software.* Addison-Wesley Professional Computing, Harlow, Essex.

Granovetter, M. S. (1973) The strength of weak ties. *American Journal of Sociology,* 73, 1360–1380.

Giddens, A. (1993) *Sociology.* 2nd edition. Polity Press, London.

Hall, E. T. (1981) *The Silent Language.* Anchor Books/Doubleday, New York (First edition, 1959).

Hall, E. T. (1983) *The Dance of Life: The Other Dimension of Time.* Anchor Press/ Doubleday, New York.

Hall, E. T. (1989) *Beyond Culture.* Anchor Books/Doubleday, New York (First edition, 1976).

Hoecklin, L. (1998) *Managing Cultural Differences. Strategies for Competitive Advantage.* Addison-Wesley Longman, Harlow, Essex.

Hoffmann, S. (2003) Start-up Phase – Einer Modernen Automobilproduktions- stätte im Spannungsfeld: HighTech, Agrarstandort und Kulturen. Dissertation. University of Applied Science, Zwickau.

Hofstede, G. (1991) *Cultures and Organizations. Software of the Mind.* McGraw- Hill Book Company, Maidenhead.

Hofstede G. (1996) *Cultures and Organisations.* McGraw-Hill Professional Publishing, Maidenhead.

Honkela, T., Kaski, S., Kohonen, T. and Lagus, K. (1998). Self-organizing maps of very large document collections: Justification for the WEBSOM method. In Balderjahn, I., Mathar, R. and Schader, M. (eds) *Classification, Data Analysis, and Data Highways.* pp 245–252. Springer Verlag, Berlin. websom.hut.fi/ websom/.

Huck, J. H. and Goldsmith, J. A. (1996) *Ideology and Linguistic Theory: Noam Chomsky and the Deep Structure Debates.* Routledge, London.

Hutchins, E. (1995) *Cognition in the Wild.* MIT Press, Cambridge, MA.

Jaegersberg, G. (2001a) Cooperation between Saxony and Paraná. WHZ and Technical University in Brazil. A project in the automotive industry. *Wirtschaftsjournal – Special 2001 – Mobility in the market.*

Jaegersberg, G. (2001b) Fatores Interculturais na Competitividade da Cadeia de Suprimentos e Logística. Seminar Paper. CEFETPR. Curitiba. October 2001.

Jaegersberg, G., Lloyd, A. D., Dewar, R. G., Pooley, R. J. and Ure, J. (2001) Managing Socio-technical Processes in the Supply Chain. Proceedings of Supply Chain Knowledge Conference, Cranfield School of Management, Cranfield.

Jaegersberg, G. (2002) International cooperation. Joint project between Zwickau and the Technical University CEFET in Brazil in the automotive industry. *Wirtschaftsjournal – Special 2002 – Mobility in the market.*

Jaegersberg, G., Hatakeyama, K., Ure, J. and Lloyd, A. D. (2002) Leveraging regional, organizational and human resources to create competitive advan- tage: a new framework for professional development. In Jardim-Gonçalves, R. and Steiger-Garção, A. (eds) *Advances in Concurrent Engineering.* Swets and Zeitlinger, Lisse.

Jaegersberg, G. (2003) Cooperation Deutschland – Brazil in automobile and automotive supply industry. *Wirtschaftsjournal – Special 2003 – No speed limits,* 42–43.

Jaegersberg, G. and Ure, J. (2003) Inter-Regional Cluster Strategies: Enhancing the Competitiveness of the German Brazilian Automotive Supply Chain. Proceedings of 2nd Virtual Conference. Cranfield University, Cranfield 17–28 November. www.sck2003.com.

Jakobs, K. (2004) Shaping Future ICT Systems through Today's Standards Setting. Proceedings of UKAIS 2004, Glasgow, 5–7 May.

Jonassen, D. H. (1996) *Handbook of Research on Educational Communications and Technology: A Project of the Association for Educational Communications and Technology*. Macmillan, New York.

Joslyn, C. and Rocha, L. (1999) *Position Paper for the NMSU Project on Decision Structures of Socio-technical Organisations in Los Alamos National Labs*. LANL www.c3.laml.gov/~joslyn.nmsu/position.html.

Kelly, G. A. (1963) *A Theory of Personality: The Psychology of Personal Constructs*. W.W. Norton, New York.

Kogut, B. and Zander, U. (1996) What do firms do? Coordination, identity and learning. *Organization Science*, 7, 502–518.

Kruschwitz, N. and Roth, G. (1999) *Inventing organisations of the 21$^{st}$ Century: Producing Knowledge through collaboration*. Centre for Coordination Science, MIT, Sloane School of Management. Working Paper 4064-99. 21C WP (Series). 031. CCSTR. 207. URI. hdl.handle.net/1721.1/2745.

Latour, B. (1986) Visualization and cognition: Thinking with eyes and hands. *Knowledge and Society: Studies in the Sociology of Culture Past and Present*, 6, 1–40.

Latour, B. (1996) Social theory and the study of computerized work sites. In Orlikowski, W. J., Walsham, G., Jones, M. R. and DeGross, J. I. (eds) *Information Technology and Changes in Organizational Work*. Chapman & Hall, London.

Laurillard, D. (1993) *Rethinking University Teaching: A Framework for the Effective use of Educational Technology*. Routledge, London.

Lave, J. and Wenger, E. (1991) *Situated learning: Legitimate peripheral participation*. The Press Syndicate of the University of Cambridge, Cambridge.

Lesser, E. L. (2000) *Knowledge and Social Capital*. Butterworth Heinemann, Boston.

Lin, N., Cook, K. and Burt, R. S. (eds) (2001) *Social Capital. Theory and Research*. Walter, New York.

Liu, L. and Yu, E. (2003) Designing information systems in social context: A goal and scenario modelling approach. *Information Systems Journal*, 29 (2).

Lloyd, A. D., Ure, J., Cranmore, A., Dewar, R. G. and Pooley, R. (2002) Designing enterprise systems: Leveraging knowledge in a distributed pattern-building community. In Jardim-Goncalves, R., Roy, R. and Steiger-Garcao, A. (eds) *Advances in Concurrent Engineering*. Swets and Zeitlinger, Lisse.

Lucier, C. E. and Torsilieri, J. D. (1997) Why knowledge programs fail: a CEO's guide to managing learning. *Strategy & Business*, 9 (Fourth Quarter), 14–28.

Luftman, J. (2001) Assessing business-IT alignment maturity. *Communications of AIS*, 4, Article 14.

Luhmann, N. (1979) *Trust and Power*. Wiley, Chichester.

Mackenzie, D. (1999) *The Social Shaping of Technology*. Open University Press, Buckingham.

Malhotra, Y. (2000) *Knowledge Management and Virtual Organizations* (Chapter VII: Using Patterns to Capture Tacit Knowledge and Enhance Knowledge Transfer in Virtual Teams). Idea Group Publishing, Hersey, PA.

Maturana, H. and Varela, F. (1992) *The Tree of Knowledge: The Biological Roots of Human Understanding*. Shambhala Pubs, Boston.

McClelland, J. L. and Rumelhart, D. E. (eds) (1986) Parallel distributed processing: Explorations in the microstructure of cognition. Vol. 2: Psychological and biological models. MIT Press, Cambridge, MA.

McMahon, M. (1997) Constructivism and the World Wide Web–A Paradigm for Learning *ASCILITE Conference*, Curtin University, Perth.

McGreal, R. (1998) Integrated distributed learning environments (IDLES) on the Internet: A survey. *Educational Technology Review (Spring/Summer)*, 9, 25–31.

Monge, P. and Contractor, N. (2003) *Theories of Communication Network.* Cambridge University Press, Cambridge.

Mumford, E. (1983) Participative systems design: Practice and theory. *Journal of Occupational Behavior,* 4, 47–57.

Mumford, E. (2003) *Redesigning Human Systems.* IRM Press, Hershey, PA.

Nahapiet, J. and Ghoshal, S. (2000) Social capital, intellectual capital and the organizational advantage. In Lesser, E. L. *Knowledge and Social Capital.* Butterworth Heineman, Boston.

Nishiguchi, T. (2000) Fractal design: Self-organising links in supply chain management. In Von Krogh, G., Nonaka, I. and Nishiguchi, T. (eds) (2002) *Knowledge Creation.* Macmillan, London. pp199–230.

Nonaka, I. (1991) The knowledge creating company. *Harvard Business Review,* November-December, 96–104.

Nonaka, I. (1998) The concept of 'ba': Building a foundation for knowledge creation. *California Management Review,* 40 (3), 40–54.

Nonaka, I. and Nishiguchi, T. (eds) (2001) *Knowledge Emergence: Social, Technical and Evolutionary Dimensions of Knowledge Creation.* Oxford University Press, Oxford.

Novak, J. D. and Gowin. D. B. (1984) *Learning How to Learn.* Cambridge University Press, New York and Cambridge.

Orlikowski, W. (2000) Using technology and constituting structures: A practice lens for studying technology in organisations. *Organization Science,* 11 (4).

Orlikowski, W. and Iacono, C. S. (2000) The truth is not out there: An enacted view of the digital economy. In Kahin, B. and Brynjolfsson, E. (eds) *Understanding the Digital Economy: Data Tools and Research.* MIT Press, Cambridge, MA.

Orlikowski, W. (2002) Managing and Designing: Learning about Enactment. Workshop paper, MIT, May 2002, design.case.edu/2002workshop/Positions/orlikowski.doc.

Pask, G. (1975) *Conversation, Cognition and Learning: A Cybernetic Theory and Methodology.* Elsevier, Amsterdam.

Pasmore, W. A. (1988) *Designing Effective Organizations: The Sociotechnical Systems Perspective.* Wiley, New York.

Piaget, J. (1970) *The Science of Education and the Psychology of the Child.* Grossman, New York.

Pike, K. L. (1981) *Tagmemic Discourse and Verbal Art.* University of Michigan/Michigan Slavic, Ann Arbor.

Pooley, R. and Stevens, P. (1999) *Using UML* Addison-Wesley Professional, Harlow.

Prusak, L. (1997) *Knowledge in Organisations.* Butterworth Heinemann, Boston.

Robey, D. and Newman, M. (1996) Sequential patterns in information systems development: An application of a social process model, *ACM Transactions on Information Systems,* 14(1), 30–63.

Rocha, L. and Bollen, J. (2001) Biologically motivated distributed design in design principles for the immune systems and other distributed autonomous systems. In Segel, L. A. and Cohen, I. R. *Design principles for the immune System and Other Distributed Autonomous Systems.* Santa Fe Institute of Studies in the Sciences of Complexity, Oxford University Press, Oxford.

Rogers, E. M. (1986) *Communication Technology: The New Media in Society.* Free Press, New York.

Rosenhead, J. and Mingers, J. (eds.) (2001) Rational Analysis for a Problematic World Revisited: Problem Structuring Methods for Complexity Uncertainty and Conflict. Wiley, Chichester.

Salerno, M. S. and Dias, A. V. C. (1998) Novos Padrões de Relacionamento entre Montadoras e Autopeças no Brasil: algumas proposições. In *XVIII Encontro Nacional De Engenharia De Produção,* Niterói.

Sawhney, M. and Parikh, D. (2001) Where value lives in a networked world. *Harvard Business Review,* January, 175–198.

Scarbrough, H., Swan, J. and Preston, J. (1999) Knowledge Management and the Learning Organisation. *Report for the Institute of Personnel Development.* Institute of Personnel Development, London.

Schroll-Machl, S. (2002) *Die Deutschen – Wir Deutsche; Fremdwahrnehmung und Selbstsicht im Berufsleben.* Bandenhoeck & Ruprecht, Göttingen.

Schueler, G. (2002) *Supply Chain Optimierung durch Analyse der interkulturellen Zusammenarbeit zwischen Deutschland und Brasilien.* Dissertation. University of Applied Sciences, Zwickau.

Segel, L. A. and Cohen, I. R. (2001) *Design Principles for the Immune System and Other Distributed Autonomous Systems* Santa Fe Institute Studies in the Sciences of Complexity, Oxford University Press, Oxford.

Senge, P., Kleiner, A., Roberts, C., Ross, R. B. and Smith, B. J. (1994) *Fifth Discipline Fieldbook: Strategies for Building a Learning Organization.* Nicholas Brealey Publishing, London.

Shneiderman, B. (1997) *Designing the User Interface: Strategies for Effective Human-Computer Interaction.* Addison Wesley, Harlow.

Shneiderman, B. (1998) Codex Memex Genex: The Pursuit of Transformational Technologies. Proceedings of Conference on Human factors in Computing Systems, CHI 98. Los Angeles, April 1998, pp 98–99. ACM Press, New York.

Simpson, G. (1998) *Decision Making Processes in the Upstream Oil and Gas Industry: Status and Future Work.* Discussion Paper. Department of Management Studies, University of Aberdeen, Aberdeen.

Suchman, L. (1987) *Plans and Situated Actions: The Problem of Human-machine Communication.* Cambridge University Press, New York.

Taylor, J. C. and Felten, D. F. (1992) *Performance by Design: Sociotechnical Systems in North America.* Prentice-Hall, Englewood Cliffs, NJ.

Trist, E. (1981) *The evolution of socio-technical systems.* Occasional Paper #2, Ontario Quality of Working Life Centre, Toronto.

Trompenaars, F. (1993) *Riding the Waves of Culture. Understanding Diversity in Global Business.* Economist Books, London.

Ure, J., Malins, J., Cullan, L. and Stenhouse, A. (2001) *StudioSpace – Teaching and Learning in Art and Design. Designing and Evaluating a Virtual Environment for Collaborative Working.* The Robert Gordon University, Aberdeen.

Ure, J., Malins, J., Murray, P. and Jaegersberg, G. (2001) Beyond Constructivism: Generative Networked Environments. Proceedings of ALT-C 2001 Conference, Edinburgh.

Ure, J. (2002) Aligning people, processes and technology. In Jardim-Goncalves, R., Roy, R. and Steiger-Garcao, A. (eds) *Advances in Concurrent Engineering: Research and Applications.* Swets and Zeitlinger, Lisse.

Ure, J. et al. (2003) Scaffolding knowledge sharing and decision support in distributed web-based systems: A socio-technical perspective. In Jardim-Goncalves, R., Cha, J. and Steiger-Garcao, A. (eds) *Enhanced Interoperable Systems.* Swets and Zeitlinger, Lisse.

Ure, J. (2004) Mental Models as Enablers of Knowledge Sharing and Decision-making in the Design of Collaborative Networked Environments. PRO-VE Working Conference on Virtual Enterprises, *World Computer Congress 2004*, Toulouse.

Von Krogh, F. G., Nonaka, I. and Nishiguchi, T. (2000) *Knowledge Creation*. Macmillan, London.

Vygotsky, L. S. (1978) *Mind in Society*. Harvard University Press, Cambridge, MA.

Walsham, G. (2001) *Making a World of Difference: IT in a Global Context*. Wiley, Chichester.

Warne, L. (2003) *Socio-technical and Human Cognition Elements of Information*. Idea Group Publishing, Hershey, PA.

Weick, K. E. (1995) *Sensemaking in Organizations*. Sage, Thousand Oaks, CA.

Wenger, E. and Snyder, W. (2002) Communities of practice: The organizational frontier. *Harvard Business Review*, January/February, 139–145.

Williams, R. (1997a) The social shaping of a failed technology? Mismatch and tension between the supply and use of computer-aided production management. In Clausen, C. and Williams, R. (eds.) *The Social Shaping of Computer-Aided Manufacture and Computer-Integrated Manufacture*, COST A4. Luxembourg, pp. 109–130.

Williams, R. (1997b) Universal solutions or local contingencies? Tensions and contradictions in the mutual shaping of technology and work organisation. In McLoughlin, I. and Harris, M. (eds) *Innovation, Organizational Change and Technology*. ITB Press, London, pp170–185.

Williams, W. and Randall, P. (1998). *Knowledge Acquisition via the Integration of Personal Constructs and Conceptual Graphs*. PhD Dissertation. Computer Science Department, University of Alabama, Huntsville.

Woolgar, S. (2003) Social Shaping Perspectives on e-Science and e-Social Science: the case for research support. *A consultative study for the UK Economic and Social Research Council, University of Oxford*. Unpublished.

Yates, J. and Orlikowski, W. (1992) Genres of organizational communication: A structurational approach to studying communication and media. *The Academy of Management Review*, 17(2), 299–326.

Zave, P. (2001) Requirements for Evolving Systems: A Telecommunications Perspective. Proceedings of 5th IEEE International Symposium on Requirements Engineering, Toronto, Canada, 27–31 August, pp 2–9. IEEE Computer Society, Washington.

# Index

actor network theory (ANT)
definition of 69–70
social architecture and 58
adaptive structuration theory (AST),
definition of 68
adding value, in socio-technical
systems 2, 13–20, 50–51
aligning constructs and models
28–31
aligning expectations 27, *Table 3.3*
aligning knowledge and objectives, in
enterprise systems 21–32,
*Table 3.1, Table 3.2*
aligning local and global
requirements 6–8, 39–42
aligning people, processes and
technology
in extended enterprise systems 45
in a modular consortium 35–39
in supply chain 39–42
aligning social and technical systems
to create value 13–20, 50–51
strategies for 15–17
Amazon, use of web-based interface
by 15, 47
analysis techniques
social network theory 67
ANT *see* actor network theory
AST *see* adaptive structuration theory
automotive procurement, local
practice in 39–42
automotive supply chain, cross-
cultural architecture in 35–46

behaviour-shaping, cycle of 45,
*Figure 4.4*

CIE *see* Common Information
Environment
cognitive process
building technology around 15–16
conceptual architecture phase in 56
constructing and modelling action
phase in 57–58
perception phase in 55–56
stages in 54–58, *Figure 6.1*
collective fames of reference,
creating 29
Common Information Environment
(CIE) 17
common platform, using 47
community of practice (CoP) 48
concept maps 57–58, 60
conceptual architecture phase, in
cognitive process 56
construct maps 57–58, 60

constructing and modelling action
phase, in cognitive process
57–58
constructs and models, aligning 28–31
CoP *see* community of practice
coupled systems
creating value through 14
as shapers of organizational
outcomes 42, *Figure 4.3*
cross-cultural architecture
in automotive supply chain 35–46
potential for conflict in 43–45
cultural dynamics, impact on standard
business processes 41, *Table 4.1*

design, implications of socio-technical
problem for 8–11, 19, 28, 31–32,
59–60, 63–66
digital image archive 17–18, *Figure 2.2*
digital repositories
case study on 14–15
definition of xi
dynamic systems theory, social
architecture and 58

ebusiness extranet 22–27
enactment theory
definition of 69
social architecture and 58
enterprise systems
aligning knowledge and objectives
in 21–32
aligning people, processes and
technology in 45
expectations, aligning 27, *Table 3.3*
extranet
definition of xi
ebusiness, in 22–27

FIFO system, and warehousing 37–38
frame of reference
collective, creating 29
organization as 29–30, *Table 3.4*
problem itself, using 31, 32, *Table 3.5*
time and sequence as 29

global and local requirements,
aligning 6–8, 39–42
global information system, definition
of xi
grid computing, definition of xi

human information processing
systems
architecture of 53–60
interoperability in 56

incompatibility in concepts of space
and time 36–37, *Figure 4.2*
information processing systems
architecture of 53–60
in natural systems 53–54
interoperability, in human information
systems 56
intranet, definition of xi
invisible architecture, seeing
63–64

JISC *see* Joint Information Systems
Committee
Joint Information Systems Committee
(JISC) 17

knowledge
cognitive process, place in 55,
*Figure 6.1*
discovery, strategies for 18–19
leveraging back- and front-end
8–10, *Figure 1.1*
mapping 60
and objectives, aligning 21–32,
*Table 3.1, Table 3.2*

languages, shared 49
leveraging back- and front-end
knowledge 8–10, *Figure 1.1*
local and global requirements,
aligning 6–8, 39–42
local practice, in automotive
procurement 39–42

Managed Learning Environment
(MLE), definition of xi–xii
management, implications of socio-
technical problem for 8–11, 19,
28, 31–32, 59–60, 63–66
middleware
definition of xi
people as 48–49
MLE *see* Managed Learning
Environment
modular consortium
aligning people, processes and
technology in 35–39
production line architecture in
35–36, *Figure 4.1*

networks, linking technical and
human 49–50

organization, as frame of reference
29–30, *Table 3.4*

81

perception phase, in cognitive
    process 55–56
platform, common, using 47
portal
    definition of xi
    in ebusiness 21–27
problem, using as frame of
    reference 31, 32, *Table 3.5*
problem scenario, in socio-technical
    systems 5–8
production schedule, change in 43–45

risk, cutting, in socio-technical
    systems 2

Scran Learning Images 9
sense-making, strategies for 18–19
sharing
    languages 49
    spaces 49
social architecture
    socio-technical systems and 58
    theoretical approaches to 58
social network theory
    definition of 67
    social architecture and 58
social process, building technology
    around 17–18
socio-technical organization (STO)
    described 2–3
    strands in 3, *Figure 0.1*
socio-technical systems
    adding value in 2, 47–51
    cutting risk in 2
    definition of 2–3, 71
    design, implications for 10–11, 19,
        28, 31–32, 59–60, 63–66

management, implications for 10–
    11, 19, 28, 31–32, 59–60, 63–66
problem with 5–11
social architecture and 58
strands in *Figure 0.1*
strategies for value creation in 47–51
typical problem scenario 5–11
soft systems methodology (SSM)
    definition of x
    in requirements analysis 53
space and time, different concepts of
    generally, 36–37
    identifying 37–39
    incompatibility of 37, *Figure 4.2*
spaces, shared 49
SSM *see* soft systems methodology
STO *see* socio-technical organization
structuration theory
    definition of 68
    social architecture and 58
supply chain
    aligning people, processes and
        technology in 39–42
    automotive, cross-cultural
        architecture in 35–46
    definition of xi
    improvement, tools for 65, *Figure 7.1*
    systems in, standardizing 6–8
system design, tensions in 23,
    *Figure 3.1*
systems theory
    definition of 70

'TalkMine' Digital Library Project 14–
    15
terrorist communication data, analysis
    of 18–19

time and sequence, used as organizing
    framework 29
time, and space, different concepts of
    generally 36–37
    identifying 37–39
    incompatibility 37, *Figure 4.2*
tools
    implications for 64–66
    supply chain improvement, for 65,
        *Figure 7.1*
training, implications for 64–66

UML *see* unified modelling language
unified modelling language (UML)
    definition of x
    in requirements analysis 53

value, creating
    by aligning social and technical
        systems 13–20, 50–51
    from both ends of network 9
    obstacles to 50–51
    in socio-technical systems 2, 47–51
    through coupled systems 14
VLE
    definition of xixii
    leveraging knowledge by means of 9

warehousing, FIFO system and 37–38
Web-based Self-Organizing Map
    (WebSOM) 15–17, *Figure 2.1*, 47
WebSOM *see* Web-based Self-
    Organizing Map

## BCS Products and Services

Other products and services from the British Computer Society, which might be of interest to you include:

### *Publishing*

BCS publications, including books, magazine and peer-review journals, provide readers with informed content on business, management, legal, and emerging technological issues, supporting the professional, academic and practical needs of the IT community. Subjects covered include Business Process Management, IT law for managers and transition management. **www.bcs.org/publications**

### *BCS Professional Products and Services*

The BCS promotes the use of the SFIA*plus* IT skills framework which forms the basis of a range of professional development products and services for both individual practitioners and employers. This includes BCS Skills*Manager* and BCS Career*Developer*. **www.bcs.org/products**

### *Qualifications*

**Information Systems Examination Board** (ISEB) qualifications are the industry standard both here and abroad, and with over 100,000 practitioners now qualified, it is proof of their popularity. They ensure that IT professionals develop the skills, knowledge and confidence to perform to their full potential. There is a huge range on offer covering all major areas of IT. In essence, ISEB qualifications are for forward looking individuals and companies who want to stay ahead – who are serious about driving business forward. **www.iseb.org.uk**

    **The BCS Professional Examination** is examined to the academic level of a UK honours degree and is the essential qualification for a career in computing and IT. Whether you seek greater job recognition, promotion or a new career direction, you will find that the BCS Professional Examination is internationally recognised, flexible and suited to the needs of the IT industry. **www.bcs.org/exam**

    **European Certification of IT Professionals** (EUCIP) is aimed at IT Professionals and Practitioners wishing to gain professional certification and competency development. **www.bcs.org/eucip**

    **European Computer Driving Licence** ™ (ECDL) is the internationally recognised computer skills qualification which enables people to demonstrate their competence on computer skills. ECDL is managed in the UK by the BCS. ECDL Advanced has been introduced to take computer skills certification to the next level and teaches extensive knowledge of particular computing tools. **www.ecdl.co.uk**

*Networking and Events*

The BCS's national network of branches and specialist groups enables members to exchange ideas and keep abreast of latest developments. **www.bcs.org/sg**

The Society's programme of social events, lectures, awards schemes, and competitions provides more opportunities to network.
**www.bcs.org/events**

*Further Information*

This information was correct at the time of publication, but could change in the future. For the latest information, please contact:

The British Computer Society,
1 Sanford Street,
Swindon, Wiltshire,
SN1 1HJ, UK.
Telephone: +44 (0) 1793 417 424
E-mail: bcs@hq.bcs.org.uk
Web: **www.bcs.org**